POSSESS THE THRONE

POSSESS THE THRONE

A YOUNG MAN'S GUIDE
TO IDENTITY AND KINGSHIP

JULIEN L. MITCHELL

authorHOUSE®

AuthorHouse™ UK Ltd.
1663 Liberty Drive
Bloomington, IN 47403 USA
www.authorhouse.co.uk
Phone: 0800.197.4150

Published by AuthorHouse 06/18/2014

ISBN: 978-1-4969-8354-1 (sc)
ISBN: 978-1-4969-8355-8 (e)

Library of Congress Control Number: 2014910722

CONTENTS

"This is the book every young man should read. It is thorough, on the mark, and very relevant. The topics covered speak directly to the heart of every young man. I wish I had the opportunity to read something like this as a teenager."

Rev. Doyle St Louis
Senior Pastor, All Nation Church of God
Springfield, MA

"I enjoyed reading this book. It opened my eyes to who I really am. It has given me the courage to be myself and reminded me that I am someone important."

Elijah Stewart
Age 19
Student

"As a mother raising all boys, it was important for me to understand the way they think. This book is a great read. It has great little nuggets of wisdom I can pass on to my sons. It straddles the line of the spiritual and the secular expertly, which makes it relatable to anyone. It has also given me the strength as a parent to know I am responsible for raising not just men, but kings."

Maria Capehart
University Lecturer of Social Science
Mother of four boys

To

Mum and Dad,

As examples go, you two were the finest. Thank you.

To

Jade,

*The best human being on the planet. When no
one else got it, you did. My sister and friend.*

To

Daniel, David, Matthew, Shem, Keeran,
Chris, Aaron, and Jermaine,

*Truly I stand in the presence of kings. Our bond knows
no depth. I cannot thank you all enough for how you all
stood by me in the most difficult moment of my life.*

To

Reverend Dr C. T. Wallace,

The greatest pastor found anywhere on the earth.

To

Reverend Dave Robinson,

*Every young man needs a "Dave" in his life. Thank
you for your mentorship, counsel, and love.*

To

Mya Lynda McTaggart,

*You are my child. You bring out my absolute best. I
just want you to be proud of me. Uncle loves you.*

1. **king** [king]. **noun** a male sovereign or monarch; a man who holds by life tenure, and usually by hereditary right, the chief authority over a country and people.

Public Service Announcement: *The rulers are back.*

For too long, our young men have been stereotyped, marginalised, and cast down. They have been unfairly criticised, harshly judged, and quickly forgotten about. No one seems to care about their real strengths and gifts; they are pushed aside and made to feel like their real home is on a sports field, on a stage in front of a microphone, or on television for the entertainment of the rich.

They are always reminded of the past and are made to feel they cannot recover from it.

They have been handed a 'manual of masculinity' by society which is full of terrible advice:

"Stop crying!"

"Man up!"

"Grow a pair!"

"Stop snitching!"

"Stop being weak!"

"Be a man and get laid!"

"Always remember: bros before hoes!"

Our young men are emotionally blunt. They are determined not to show any of that emotion in the event the river dam of the heart breaks and everything that has been suppressed for years comes pouring out.

On the outside, they have done a great job in concealing their issues. They wear the mask, and they wear it well. It seems crazy to think these same young men we see are struggling with an identity for themselves. The exterior exudes arrogance, self-assurance, and egotistical behaviour, but this exterior only exists because the interior is deeply flawed. On the inside, our boys are scared. They are hurting, they are doubting themselves, they are vulnerable.

Role models are few and far in between. These youthful gentlemen are simply going through life, "winging it."

There is no need to begin to go into the facts and figures of unemployment, incarceration, and education performance. The truth is that there is progress in these areas, but the standard must be lifted back to the place where it is supposed to be.

I refuse to believe that our bright, sensitive, beautiful young men are just what they appear to be. I refuse to believe that all they aspire to is posing for pictures with champagne bottles in a club, I refuse to believe that they enjoy a life of crime and actively persue it, and I refuse to believe that they will willingly put their image above their integrity, but I do believe a change is coming.

I believe our men are getting ready to take their place back. I believe they will acquire the knowledge that will open their eyes to see what real strength and masculinity is. I believe that there is a remnant of young boys who will rise to the mark that is set for them. I believe there is soon to be a wave of polished young sirs who will grow tired of being average and see no delight in attention seeking but take joy in self-respect, chivalry, and obtaining intelligence.

As we speak, our future prime minister may be struggling with his identity. Our future leaders may be having a hard time making friends and fitting in. Our future owners and bosses are about to face a judge who wants to make an example out of them. We cannot give up on our boys.

Let's point them towards the throne, their throne. Let them take a seat. Allow them to adjust and get comfortable. Let's blow the trumpets and signal their arrival. This is their rightful place. This is where they belong.

I declare our young men shall be victorious. The rulers are back. The kings are here. Death to the pseudo-image of male identity, long live the kings!

My name is Julien Mitchell. This has been a public service announcement.

OVERTURE

This is for you.

This is for the young man like myself. The one with the crown under the snapback, the one whose confidence is hidden and strengths are misplaced. This is for the one who is still learning. The one who can't find his feet in a bedroom full of sneakers, the one who triumphs in the victory of finding approval. This is for the one who is acquainted with anxiety, distinguished in disappointment, identifies with insecurity, and knows the indication of isolation.

This is for the one who is oblivious to his throne. The one who is unaware of his importance, the one who cannot fathom his destiny.

I wrote this for the countless number of young men like myself. This is for the one who finds growing up difficult. This is for the one who just isn't sure who, or what, he is supposed to be.

This is the book I wish someone had given to me when I was a young teenager. I write this book so life no longer becomes an aimless walk, trying to find the needle in the haystack.

This is a book written to help you finally understand *you*.

This is a guide of how you handle life's side roads when who you are has eventually become clear to you.

My hope and prayer for you is that you will finally begin to look at yourself through the eyes of your creator, that your identity is no longer a mystery to you, and at the close of this guide, that you will feel a renewed sense of purpose and destiny for your life.

Not everything will be applicable to you, but there is something, somewhere in this book, that will ask questions of you.

This book has nine separate phases; they each represent an area of life that I, and plenty of other men have struggled with at some point. Each phase offers advice for you to digest and make adjustments in your life if, and where necessary.

Much is expected of you. There are people counting on you. I'm sure you're able to tell me why you can't succeed; this book is here to tell you why you can.

I'm simply here to tell you that there is a king in you, because that's who you are.

This is for you. Enjoy.

Phase I

I Am King

"The beginning of wisdom is to call things by
their right names."

Chinese proverb

I am a lover of all things comedy. Stand-ups, sitcoms, you name it. It was only natural that in the springtime of 2003, I had to catch the latest Adam Sandler movie: *Anger Management*. This movie is centred on Dave Buznick, a humble businessman played by Sandler, who is wrongly accused of having anger issues. As a relative of mine and I sat in the movie theatre, unable to contain our laughter from the outset, a particular scene arrested my attention and sent my thought processes into overdrive.

Dave attends his first anger management session, where his therapist, Dr Buddy Rydell, played by Jack Nicholson, warmly welcomes him to the group. After Dr Rydell's introduction, he asks, "Who are you?"

Dave begins to tell the group about his current employment, to which Dr Rydell interrupts and points out that he does not want to hear about what he does, but rather "who he is."

Dave regroups his thoughts and proceeds to tell the group some of the things he likes to do in his spare time. Again, Dr Rydell stops him in mid-sentence and reminds Dave that he is sharing his hobbies, while he wants an answer to the question "Who are you?"

Dave struggles to find an acceptable answer. He starts to describe his personality. For the third time, Dr Rydell cuts in and tells Dave that it is not his personality he is interested in hearing about, and he patronisingly asks him again to answer the question. At this point, Dave's frustration takes over, and he reacts angrily at his inability to find what a reasonable response would be.

As I sat in the theatre, I tried my very best to answer this question for myself. Seems simple enough, right? The truth is, I would have probably answered that question the same way Dave did.

Dr Rydell, however, was absolutely correct in reminding Dave that his occupation, his hobbies, and his personality are not justifiable answers. Many would argue that an accumulation of these things would result in an absolute definition of who you are. I disagree. That method of thought walks right alongside the "You are what you eat" theory, and while I support aspects of that theory, I do not believe it applies here.

Who you are is not found in what you do. We can very easily make the mistake and melt the two together. Individuals can work for years for that dream job and feel a huge sense of accomplishment when they obtain it. God forbid they ever lose that job; the natural feeling that proceeds is to think they have lost who they are if they have allowed what they do to become one with their identity. The truth is, they have lost a job, not themselves. The same goes for our hobbies and even our personalities. Things change; who we are should not.

Having said that, the question remains, who are you?

The Bible stands as one of the most coherent sources that explicitly tells you who you are.

*"But **you are** a chosen generation, a royal priesthood, a holy nation, His own special people, that you may proclaim the praises of Him who called you out of darkness into His marvellous light."*

1 Peter 2:9

Scripture gives us a wonderful, undiluted, almost inconceivable picture of who we are. Chosen. Royal. Holy. Different. This is the very image of you. For the sake of this dissertation, I want to focus on this notion of *royalty*. How and why are we defined with such an illustrious, noble, and renowned title?

Usually, to be known as royalty is hereditary. It is a right that is held through family. A king is a king because his father was a king.

Our heavenly father stands as the supreme, sovereign King. Jesus is known as the King of Kings. We have this right to call ourselves kings because by definition of being children of God, that is who we are.

With this right comes a mandate. To be privileged with such an appellation means our conduct and our behaviour must match the status.

A king has roles. A king's first role is a ruler. He holds responsibility over a group of people, family, or clan. A king is a man of war, both in the natural and the spiritual. He is the source of identification, a model to relate to, someone to copy and (in today's society) to hate. A king has a moral obligation to set the standard and can never fall victim to compromise.

You are called to rule. To rule is to possess and control everything that is at your immediate disposal. Your time, your money, your emotions, your actions, your words are all yours to seize complete dominance over. It becomes dangerous to lose control over anything you have the right to own.

You are called to protect your family. Your brothers and sisters, your mother, your sons and daughters, your aunts, your cousins, everyone in the clan. It is your role to look out for them. Be mindful, young man, that your mother is still your mother; you are not to rule her, you are to protect her.

You are called to war. In your case, to war is to fight for a just cause. The uncompromising king stands and supports what he believes in. You are a defender of those who need defending and a voice for those who do not have one. Your weapons are not your fists but rather your actions. Prayer is your most valuable source of ammunition.

You are called to be placed on a platform. Hate it or love it, someone is watching you. Some with good intentions, some with intentions to harm. Many will want to see and celebrate your success, others will want to gloat and revel in your failures. You will have those who are waiting for you to demonstrate your identity, and those who cannot wait to use your identity against you. Keep your responses to naysayers to a minimum; this is how character is built.

If, brother, you are to walk in your rightful identity of a king, these are some of the roles that come with the territory. You must first understand that what is required of you is required by all, but only understood by a few. Regardless of race, culture, income, and family background, it is the call of every male to bear this position of distinction.

The wonderful thing about knowing your identity as a king is that it gives you a focus while travelling the road of self-discovery. Knowing who you are supposed to be, and shaping your character to get there, is a far more satisfying journey than attempting to figure out who you are and ultimately settling for a watered-down version of the true essence of your existence. Your true identity shows no respect to age. Your kingship was established on the day of your birth, and it sits patiently as it waits for you to fig. ure out that this throne belongs to you.

To walk unequivocally in your identity as a king takes time. The aim here is not to get you to a particular stage in life without the aid of experience and maturity, but rather to lay the blueprint of transition between understanding who you are and eventually walking boldly in it. Think of it like this: a company has just hired you as chairman, not employee, not manager, but the big cheese himself. You are thrown straight into the deep end without any training, tutelage, or instruction. Sounds daunting, doesn't it?

Well, the good thing about this particular company is that they are willing to give you the role now and let you figure out how to operate in it later. If it takes you nine years, nineteen years, or ninety, what does not change is the fact that you *are* the chairman. The title is yours, the role belongs to you, and no one can take it away from you. The decision now lies with you in determining what kind of chairman you want to be. Your training will be tough, but if you wish to become as accomplished as you can in your role, you must become accustomed to how a chairman functions. Once that is understood, you're free to resume the hot seat in your own way.

The same goes for your rightful identity as a king. It is God-given DNA. It is already in you to become ruler, but the process must take place. It is a challenging one, but one you can successfully accomplish.

Now is probably a good time to point out that there is no outcome of perfection here. What I am not saying is with the realisation of your identity comes this perfect man who has reached his zenith in life and has nothing left to learn. You do not need me to tell you that no one is perfect. You can retrace the steps of history and see there is a tremendous number of monarchs of this world who have had the status but were let down by their poor decisions, their bad habits, their greed, and even their lusts of the flesh. None of these men were spotless or untarnished, but they were kings, and their apparent flaws did not change that.

Figuring out your identity as a king does come with a sense of what your decorum and attitude ought to be. Given the reality that there are some things that appear taboo for a king to do, on your scale, that reality is the same. For example, the media attention that surrounded Prince Harry during his trip to Las Vegas in 2012 for seemingly doing what "normal" young men do when abroad with friends is an ideal spotlight that those of royalty will be scrutinised for what is seen as "out-of-character" behaviour. Although, let me be clear, this does not mean that you are not allowed to have fun. But whatever your definition of "fun" is, you must do it without being reckless. Be responsible, and hold yourself accountable at all times.

Whether you realise it or not, there is a king in you. The standard for you as the complete man has been set. The acceptable position of royalty belongs to you. Who you are is no longer defined in what you do, what you wear, and all that other jazz, but who you are is defined by the fact that you are God's son, and with that fact, there is a mark to meet. This mark is not to say that you will become superior to your peers, but it is there so you can no longer walk in confusion about your identity.

You are a king. It is time to refer to yourself accordingly.

Let's continue.

Phase II

WHO? ME?

"Uneasy lies the head that wears a crown."

William Shakespeare

Football has always been a passion of mine. I have watched, played, studied, and analysed the game I love with much intent. My father recognised my passion for the sport from an early age and endeavoured to find a team for me to play on. It so happened on a particular afternoon he came across an advert for a local team holding tryouts for ten- to thirteen-year-olds. Being left handed also meant I was very much left footed, which is exactly what this particular team was after. My father took me to the trials, and on the same day, the coach offered me a spot on the team. I did not sign a contract, I had no endorsement deal, I did not receive a signing on fee, and I did not have any interviews, but I could not have felt more like a professional footballer if I tried. Dad bought me my first pair of boots and my first pair of shin pads, and that was it. In my mind, I was a footballer, and you could not tell me otherwise.

The team I played for were not very good. If truth be told, we were awful in our first few games, but we grew to understand each other's strengths and weaknesses, and we slowly got better. As far as a Sunday league football team went for young boys, my team had no money whatsoever. We had to pay two pounds to attend training sessions on Friday evening and three to play on match days on

Sunday. Our coach was very strict and always repeated, "If you don't pay, you don't play."

At halftime during a game, both teams would sit out on the field, and we would always look over at the other teams with envy as they drank out of the blue Lucozade bottles we saw the professionals use and eat chocolate energy bars, while we would share around the plastic cups, eating Satsuma's and drinking diluted orange squash provided by someone's mother. Every other team in the league had new shirts and shorts to play in every year, while we played in the same uniform for three seasons.

We were not a glamorous team by any stretch of the imagination, but I did not want to play for anyone else. I was the only legitimate left-footed player and the only black player too. I wore this as a badge of honour. To me, it meant I stood out from everyone else, and I was quickly singled out as one of the best on the team. I realised this during halftime of a game on a sweltering hot Sunday afternoon, when I overheard the mother of a team-mate say to my father, "Your Julien is one of our star players."

I knew I was important to the team, and I knew to some degree how well the team performed very much depended on how I performed. However, during one particular summer, the team literally fell apart. A disagreement happened between the coach and the parents of some of the players, and one by one they began taking their boys out of the team. It got to the extent where the team only had two registered players: me and the son of the coach. We were excluded from the upcoming season but began to rebuild. We saw an influx of new boys come into the team, and soon we were a squad again, albeit a new, unrecognisable one. The talent and the standard of the new team was now way higher than the previous one, to the extent it became very clear to me that I was no longer the best. I was no longer the only left footer on the team, I was no longer the only black player either, and in a strange way, all the things that I believed made me special to this team I was now sharing with others. My performance began to suffer, my starting place in the team was now threatened, and I began to question the confidence I had in my own ability. On a cold, rainy Sunday morning, I turned in one of the worst performances of my life. I was being shouted at by my team-mates, my head went down, and the coach had enough sense to put me out of my misery and hauled me out of the game. As I sat pitch side on the wet, muddy grass, the coach kneeled down next to me and said, "You won't be playing next week, or the week after." In that sobering moment, I had forgotten all of the good games I played, I had forgotten about my ability, and all I saw before me was a boy, in a jersey two sizes too big for him, who is probably not as good as he thinks he is.

I had lost all motivation to play the game I once loved. My opinion of myself as a footballer went from ten to zero in an instant. My team-mates would say I was terrible, and I believed them, and because I believed them, I began playing like it. The thought of "not good enough" firmly resided in my mind. And to make matters worse, the players who I thought were better than me now intimidated me, all because of the thoughts I thought towards myself.

As a teen, that thought of "not good enough" is a dream killer. It has no problem in reminding you that you do not have what it takes to succeed. It is happy to let you know that there are too many out there who are more capable, more talented, and more suited for the job. The truth is, we all at some stage, whether as a teenager or as a grown adult, will have feelings of inadequacy.

This feeling can put us in a sober and subdued state, where we begin to rethink our capability, and it can make us lose both our desire and will. The terrible thing about experiencing inadequacy is that it is extremely forgetful. A moment of self-deficiency will not jog your memory about how good you once were, or what you once thought about yourself. It gives a damning verdict of the present. It makes the past count for nothing and the future seems pointless. Maybe it's me, but have you ever had someone, maybe a parent, a guidance councillor, or a friend, give you a diagnostics of your life and tell you this is what you are good at and this is what you can become, and you think to yourself, *What are you talking about?* What they said is so far off the mark of what you think your ability is. If anyone knows you well, it is you. You are the one who is aware of your resourcefulness and is mindful of your own faculty, right? I thought like that too.

Sometimes, people can see things in us that we cannot for ourselves, or it could just be we choose not to see them because our apparent flaws are all too real and evident for our potential to really matter. When it comes to our own self-development, we can occasionally be too hard on ourselves. We can be pessimistic about our chances to succeed because of various things, but the majority of them will have something to do with the kind of person we think we are, or what we think are capable of. Our opinions of ourselves are a general way of discovering our level of self-esteem.

Sometimes, to possess little self-regard can be down to many factors. Negative life experiences are often contributors to low self-esteem and can give us an unfavourable overall conclusion of who we think we are. To know who you are is to know who you are not; this is one of the first stages to address when boosting low self-esteem and banishing the thoughts of "not good enough."

Our behaviour has a strange way of convincing us that there is a connection to what we do and who we are. We often think we have become what we do, because why would we do it, if that is not who we are? Get it? To simplify, I defined myself as a terrible footballer because I played terrible. When the truth is, I happened to be a good footballer who had a terrible game. Had I reminded myself of this fact, inadequacy would not have eaten away at me, and I would not see those who appeared to be better than me become a threat, because I already knew how good I can be. How good they are, or their opinion of how good they think I am, should not change how good I *know* I am.

We have a habit as human beings to address and define ourselves and other people by their behaviour. For example, someone is known as a thief if they are caught stealing; this does not mean a thief is who they are, but thieving is what they have done. Behaviour is activity, *not* identity. Having said that, I can imagine it can appear strange for a young man to be told he can walk around with the status of a king, knowing what his behaviour is like, especially if it is of the nature that many will generally frown upon. Allow me to address this. Whenever you put your behaviour before your identity, most of the time you will think that your identity is out of reach because of some of the things you have done in the past, so this thought may immediately spring to mind: *How can I be known as a king if I've done so many negative things?*

Thinking this way will have your behaviour (what you do, or what you have done) begin to dictate who you are, and as a result, it becomes hard to see past your apparent mistakes. Here is where you have to do your best to flip that way of thinking. Instead of putting your behaviour before your identity, put your identity before your behaviour. Allow *who you are* to dictate *what you do.* When you are mindful that there is a crown on your head, and there is a status you must live up to, that in itself can alter the opinion you may have of yourself and adjust your behaviour to one that reflects your identity.

Low self-esteem can come from the negative responses shown by the world when they see things such as your skin colour or your physical stature, but it is important that when you look in the mirror, you see your own positive opinion of you, rather than a negative opinion that other people share. It is okay to have a good, definitive evaluation of yourself, and no matter what, stand by your evaluation. "It's not what they call you, it's what you answer to" without a doubt applies here. Hold control of your self-esteem by choosing to ignore what people say about you. Answering or challenging these people implies you have accepted those labels, which takes the control of your self-esteem out of your hands. A king is someone who sticks by his guns and is not thrown off by the murmuring and whispers of everyone else. A king will let them talk, for he is far too busy attending to matters much more important.

Having self-love is important, but too much of it is damaging to your character. This is not high self-esteem, it is narcissism. What you do not want to do is to begin to think you are above correction, which can trap you into a false sense of entitlement and leave you with the inability to learn from your mistakes. Hold yourself in high regard, but not too high where you become unrecognisable to everyone else.

We all have flaws, and we all think we have reasons for not wanting to do better, but actually our reasons are just excuses. Do not fall into the habit of making excuses for yourself, but rather be honest about what you think is holding you back and address it. While realising your identity as a king, it does not come with this newfound superpower that everything you once hesitated doing, for whatever reason, you will all of a sudden conquer. If you hate public speaking, you will still hate public speaking, even with the knowledge of who you are. Something like that takes practice and adjustment. Your identity as a king will not turn you into this captivating orator, but it will force you to view yourself a little differently in the sense of your feelings towards you as a person.

While feelings of inadequacy are not the only things that can force people to steer away from their true identity, one of the biggest and most subtle destroyers of destiny is fear. Fear is responsible for unfulfilled dreams, at fault for missed opportunities, and to blame for the feelings birthed and decisions made through the mere threat and presence of failure, pain, rejection, and danger. It is controlling and manipulating.

A common, real fear amongst young people is the fear of unfulfilled potential. It is the intention of youth leaders, advisors, and mentors everywhere to instil a belief in the young that anything is possible, and nothing is out of reach. While that is absolutely true and sound advice, I can understand it can be a slightly overwhelming feeling to be told that you possess this unbelievable potential to be greater and go further than anyone has done before. On young shoulders, this weight of expectation can become a burden. Young people realise quickly the pressure of being placed in such a high place that even one step below where they ought to be can be a disappointment to so many.

These young people are often the victims of their parents' dead dreams. From an early age, their parents will push them into activities and force an unhealthy work ethic on them. This "failure is not an option" mentality will have you believing that the world has come to an end and there is no longer a reason to live when failure eventually arrives.

The question stands at this point: What do you expect from yourself? A wise lady once told me, "You must eat the fish and spit out the bones," meaning you can listen to everyone else's evaluation of you, about what you can and cannot do, but it is your choice what you accept and what you reject. Having heard what others have to say, how is your own assessment of your own potential in your own mind pieced together? How far can you go? How successful can you be?

The answer to those questions is solely up to you. What is important is you do not become overly concerned with what everyone else thinks. No one can run your race for you; no one can dictate what pace you ought to go at. You have one life to live, and you will not make progress if your concentration is centred on what you cannot do. No longer should you be afraid of failure. Failure will teach you things that no lecturer or book can ever teach. over 150 years ago, William Edward Hickson said it best: "If at first, you don't succeed, try try again."

What you must do, however, is develop a mind that says as long as you are willing to put the effort in, nothing is out of your reach. If you want it, go and get it. If you think it is worth the fight, the energy, and the discouragement that comes in the pursuit, then keep your head down, and eventually the achievement will be yours. Let your heart's desire be genuine, and let your intention keep you focused.

Kings are those who make it happen. They put their dreams before their fears. They understand that while everyone else can say no, all they need is a yes from themselves. They are aware of their potential and have no doubt in their ability. A king is one who cultivates what he is good at and works hard on what he lacks. He practices like the worst and performs like the best. He stands against pessimism and refuses to blow balloons for a pity party when things do not go according to plan.

Trust yourself. You will not always get things right, but you must refuse to listen to the nagging voices that want to remind you how wrong you were. There is something about *you,* yes, you, that has something to offer. Someone somewhere needs to benefit from what you bring to the table. Let experience be your teacher, allow God to design your pathway, be confident in your capacity, and remind fear and doubt about who you are.

Phase III

THE DILEMMA OF THE DISTINCTIVE

"And Adoni-Bezek said, 'Seventy Kings with their thumbs and big toes cut off used to gather scraps under my table; as I have done, so God has repaid me."

Judges 1:7

S haun Ross is one of the most successful male fashion models in recent times. He is currently best known as being the first mainstream male albino model. Born from African American parents, Ross began his foray in the world of modelling at the age of sixteen and has since worked with some of the biggest fashion brands and some of the most popular publications in the world. During a talk show interview in 2009, Ross revealed intimate details about his troubled childhood. He spoke about being the only light-skinned person in an entire school of over six hundred black and Hispanic students in New York, and how he was bullied because of his albinism. He was singled out by his peers because he looked different, and he found it extremely hard to fit in and find his way during his adolescent years.

Ross recalled an incident where he was involved in an altercation with another student who called him "bread." This same student stabbed Ross in his back six times with a sharp pencil, each wound being six inches deep. Ross talked about knowing he was "different" when he reached his teenage years, where he was beaten up almost every day and was a constant target for bullies. Eventually, he said, he learnt to accept himself, that there was not a way to fit in and stay true to himself, and in order to be happy, he had to embrace his difference.

The self-doubt Shaun Ross experienced as a teenager is an awareness countless number of young people all over the world have experienced, including me. Few have had to endure what Ross has, but many know something about not fitting in; they know something about what separation from a crowd feels like. Looking back on my adolescent years, and reminiscing on my school days, you had two choices: You either stood out, or you joined in. We all in some way, even at a young age, have a sense of what we want and what we like. We know what we will tolerate, we know how far is too far, and we know when to draw the line. Unfortunately, we are willing to put the knowledge of these things aside if they do not line up with the way of thinking from the majority.

There were always the brave few who were willing to stick to what they knew and did not compromise, regardless of how strong the force from the masses was as an opposition. These few were the bullied, the tormented, the persecuted, and the tortured, simply for being themselves. There were those who refused to go through the oppression, and those who dedicated themselves to conform and merge with a set of views, values, and opinions they do not share. They adopted a vernacular that was once foreign; they accommodated a behaviour they knew would not be tolerated at home and attuned a mentality that was not justified.

This was me. I did all those things that I was not comfortable with, but as long as I was not being bullied, as long as I was popular, as long as I stayed on trend, knowing I was being someone I was not was worth it, or so I thought. I can imagine in schools and colleges across many nations, to be a part of a particular group was almost like a rite of passage; it was a level of acceptance that was seen as a holy grail for many teenagers. As I reminisce on those eventful days, I see how focused I was to be a part of something that was never intended for me. I tried everything to belong, and it worked for the most part, but only to my detriment.

What was interesting was the young men who were a part of this elite, or clique that all respected, feared, and wanted to be associated in some way with, moved more like an organisation than a group of friends. Young men will walk in groups. The exposure of moving alone is too hot, so they would rather remain low key and under the radar in a crowd. Every single day after school, a group of us, sometimes as large as thirteen young men, would walk leisurely to McDonald's and just sit in the restaurant. Thirteen teenagers who dressed the same, talked the same, and walked the same made a habit of just hanging around, for no apparent reason other than just to do it. Someone might order a cheeseburger, and someone else would ask for a cup of water, but out of thirteen, only two would be eating. The rest of us just sat and watched people go in and out of the restaurant.

At the time, we looked cool; we walked in numbers, and no one would trouble us. We had the same conversation every day, and we were happy doing this, because conformity brought a comfort and a security that our individualism could not provide. In hindsight, we wasted so much time lounging in a random fast food restaurant and did little to justify ourselves as anything other than loud, aggressive teenagers.

Many young people will do what they can to be respected and admired by their peers, and regrettably, we live in a culture that makes following the crowd seem compulsory. We will go in whichever direction the wind blows. It is striking when we see so many of our young men with absolutely no sense of individualism. Society continues to churn out this generic young person from a conveyer belt and, in the process, convinces these young minds that acceptance is found in the masses. If the truth is told, our youth currently live within an education system that does not make it easy to embrace their individualism. Everyone is expected to learn and develop in the same way, and everyone is graded in like manner. Opportunities are limited if you do not meet the standard that the curriculum has set. This is an unfair base to judge the intelligence or capabilities of our young people.

We must understand that the capacity to be taught varies from each individual. To count someone out because their grades were not as good as another person's is like telling a fish he will not amount to anything because he cannot climb a tree the way a monkey can. A fish can do things that a monkey cannot do, but we fail to spot individual strength. These strengths are never nurtured and matured in our youth, and we give them no other option but to think that they must do as everyone else, think like everyone else, and be like everyone else in order to succeed. The mindset of looking for approval in achievement rather than looking for approval from within is now established, and so many will not do unless it has been done before, will not say unless it has been said before, and will not think unless someone has thought of it first. We now have a generation who would rather follow than lead. They would rather re-invent the wheel and stay on trend rather than set one.

Trends are important to those who do not understand that they can create a lane for themselves. To do as everyone else does is the only option when you do not realise the choice is there to discover your identity.

We have young kings walking around like paupers, shadows of their true selves. Too many are willing to settle for common conversation and average activity with passable people. Many young men are fixing for an uninspired life they were never called to live. It is a sad state of affairs when we witness a large quantity of young males with a chip on their shoulders, some due to insecurities that have not been addressed, others due to the appeal of playing a role. Either way, that life was never intended to be their portion.

To conform to the habits of the majority is the easiest way to get lost in a crowd. It is far more damaging than just mimicking urban vernacular or purchasing a type of footwear that a celebrity has been seen in, but your entire thought process runs parallel with what everyone else thinks, without you having an input of your own. To desire to be accepted by a group means you must accept their ideology, which leaves no room for you to think and act for yourself. This has become a major struggle in the lives of so many young men, especially those who continue with the pursuit to find where exactly their place is in a social environment.

The overwhelming pressure on young people today to experience acceptance and acknowledgement can sometimes make them lose all sense of their uniqueness. To recognise you are unique is a step in the right direction to gaining an understanding of your identity. To understand your identity and to walk in it releases you from the stronghold of conformity. Breaking away from conformity makes the masses look at you as different (which you are) and ultimately might land you in the arena of dislike. Distressingly, but in some ways understandably so, the burden of being an outcast is too great a weight to bear in the life of an adolescent man, and it begins to outweigh the importance of self-discovery.

In the Old Testament book of Judges, scripture portrays for us a striking resemblance of troubled kings today. Adoni-Bezek was an evil Canaanite king who had a reputation for cutting off the thumbs and the big toes of other kings he defeated in battle. Eventually, Adoni-Bezek was caught, and under the Mosaic law of "an eye for an eye," he suffered the same fate as his victims. His reason for cutting off the thumbs and big toes of the kings was in a way very clever. This rendered them ineffective as warriors. Without thumbs, they could not hold their weapons, and without big toes, they could not run.

In a strange way, a similar figurative consequence is happening to the young kings of today, living without "thumbs" and "big toes." They are living in a state of being unfruitful and unproductive. Having a young man with this mindset of worthlessness is like having a car with no wheels. This mindset will have him question his purpose. He has no thumbs, so he struggles to hold on to anything.

He struggles to hold on to what he believes, he finds it difficult to hold on to his opinion, and he can have his mind easily manipulated. He will buckle under the first sign of pressure from his peers who want him to do as they do, and he will do it while feeling uncomfortable about it. He has no big toes, so he finds it hard to make any real movements of purpose. He has an issue with a vision for himself and adopts a "go with the flow" attitude. Your big toes are also what you need for balance. Where there is no balance in one's life, there is often chaos. Life moves from spontaneous to out of control, because there is no evidence of consistency or stability. Without his thumbs and big toes, this young king now stands in a state of vulnerability and becomes an easy target.

When Adoni-Bezek is finally arrested, he tells his captors that the same thing they have done to him is the same thing he has done to seventy kings. Not only has he removed the thumbs and big toes of these men, but he keeps them underneath his table. This gives us a desperately shocking and direful image of these kings. Men once of stature and valour, now without the ability to hold on or to run, and are dumped under the table of the enemy, sharing space with dogs and looking for scraps of food to eat.

It makes for very depressing reading and an even more depressing reality when today's kings are not far off this state of trouble.

A great number of our young kings are currently underneath the table. They are in places they do not belong and keeping company that does not benefit them. They have become dependent. Instead of developing a work ethic, they rely on handouts. They are too busy gathering scraps, collecting the small, insignificant, and unimportant things of this world, like cars, clothes, and money, and using these things as a sign of success and power. Under the table has become too comfortable for too many. It is a place where you are not seen or heard, where you can make no impact and have no influence. Sadly, we have young, potential-filled kings abiding in this darkest of places.

There is a dilemma that comes with being distinctive. One thing a king cannot do is fall victim to compromise. This means sometimes making the unpopular choice if he knows it will benefit others as well as himself. A king must stick to his guns and ignore the voices that wish to dictate what he does and how he does it. This is a practice our young men must adopt. There is a consequence in not doing what others want you to do, and no one wants to be unpopular for being themselves, but this is the reality of the position. It calls for strength to be you. It calls for a backbone and the courage to walk on your own road instead of joining a queue to a destination that was not intended for you.

If I had the opportunity to speak to one of the kings underneath Adoni-Bezek's table, I would ask him, what happened? How did you find yourself from the throne to occupying the space of animals? Could it be that somewhere along the line, you have forgotten who you are, or have you not yet grasped the concept of your real identity?

Even with so many young men with missing thumbs and big toes, these can effectively grow back with the realisation of who you are. You might be under the table with many others, but just because they have conformed to making it their home, you don't have to. This is the time to examine yourself and use it as the beginning to work on your exclusiveness. Do not let *you* go to waste. Attempting to live the life of a life that has been already lived is characterless. You are the best *you* that you can be, and no one can beat you at being you. As a king, you are positioned to make a difference, but you cannot make the difference without thinking in a new way. In a nutshell, your identity will not allow you to be comfortable with the familiar, once you realise who you are. Be daring to be distinctive. Too many are unnerved by the unconventional and are running scared of the radical. Let no one put limits on your gift. Too many young kings are settling for "good" and "ordinary." Don't be like the peacock, the same bird that shows his feathers in an attempt to impress others, the same bird that walks with an arrogant strut and believes he is above all other birds. This is the same bird that, for his entire decadent and attractive exterior, can't fly.

Never apologise for being peculiar. Celebrate yourself for being incomparable, unequal, and unlike. You have been selected to make changes, called to live level headed, and picked out to dream high.

To live as a king is to embrace your *sui generis*. Apply your individualism with your identity, and the quality of you as a young man will be found. Get your thumbs back. Get your big toes back.

Phase IV

ADOLESCENT LEADERSHIP

"If you think you are too small to be effective,
you have never been in bed with a mosquito."

Betty Reese

Leadership, in my view, has many misconceptions. To some, being a leader means you must become this energetic, charismatic figure who is both alluring and dominant. There are thousands of tips and tricks on the Internet that will teach you how to become an effective leader. Many of these tips discuss character traits, ways you can talk to people, never showing weakness; the list is endless. To me, this way of teaching leadership is a form of manipulation. That may seem like a strong word, but whenever you get into the arena of thinking about how you can get people to follow you, and what you can do to have people on your side, it says to me that the idea is to mould the minds of individuals rather than to inspire them.

History has given us many great examples of strong and effective leadership, but so often we look at these examples from an exterior perspective. We look at great leaders such as King Louis XIV of France, who stands as the longest serving monarch of all major countries in European history, someone who did not have much of an academic background, a man who moulded seventeenth-century France into an educated, cultivated standard for all European countries to follow. We assess King Louis XIV on how he was able to maintain the following of a people for so long. There were others, such as the Macedonian king, Alexander the Great. Undefeated in battle, created empires before his thirtieth birthday, and generally seen as one of the most ruthless and dominating rulers to have ever lived. When I look closer to home and review the life of my pastor, the Reverend Dr Cleveland Wallace, a man who has been involved in ministry for well over six decades, a man who has held on to the faith for so long, I sometimes wonder what he has that makes him such a revered leader. We marvel at the achievements and accomplishments of these men and attempt to mimic their characteristics to bring to pass a similar result when it comes to being a convincing leader.

However, to gain a sense of understanding what it takes to be a leader, we must look beyond achievement, status, and personality when making a particular character a case study. More than their dynamic and expressive display of public speaking, more than their exploits, what was it that drove these men to greatness?

The great generals of our time all shared very different and contrasting ideals, from Charlemagne to Winston Churchill, but one thing they all had in common was their powerful conviction, and how convinced they were in those ideals. These were not just men who performed from a platform, but men, regardless of what we may think of their methods and pattern, who were totally unmoved in what they believed. These were men who showed incredible fortitude and bravery to get their message across and never compromised.

You begin to realise, when analysing great leaders, that there is a shared sense of devotion to their goals. These goals were not small targets they had to meet, but life-changing moments for the people and the country they were leading. These goals were personal to these men. The great things that well-known leaders have done throughout history are in fact extensions of their minds, the very fruit which came from their core. The ideals of the great leaders of our time started from within. It was a desire, a passion, an intense eagerness that had nothing to do with self-promotion or praise, but simply to see what they believed come to pass. In truth, it does not even have anything to do with having people follow them, but this extreme ambition naturally creates a magnetism, whereby individuals are drawn to them not as people in position, but as people of purpose.

The late Nelson Mandela, for example, served time in prison over what he believed in. He famously confessed he was willing to die as long as it meant the people of his homeland could live together in harmony and with equal opportunities. Known as "the father of the nation," Mandela did not allow almost thirty years of incarceration to stop his dream of fairness and equality for his country.

For me, the fact that Mandela was the first black South African to hold the office of president in his country is noteworthy, as is the fact that he won the Nobel Prize. Neither achievement is to outweigh his ideal. His ideal of a better society is responsible for his roll of accomplishments. It is this ideal, which came from a place of personal passion for the people of South Africa, is what makes him one of the great leaders of our time.

You may wonder, "At this stage in my young life, what does leadership have to do with me?" I'm glad you asked.

In my humble opinion, leadership is two things: being a *servant*, and being an *example*.

To serve and to lead at the same time may sound like an oxymoron, but it serves as the bedrock for effective leadership.

If we can, for a second, not be too concerned with this title of "leader," but focus on this concept of having and obtaining an ideal.

What is it that drives you? What is your passion? Both are questions for any young man to begin to think about. Your passion could be a number of things: playing a sport, writing, music, your community, photography; literally anything you bear a deep and significant interest in. To cultivate your own ideal in the area of your passion is to become a servant to it. What can you do and how can you serve your passion so that it can become better? If your passion is in the industry of fashion, what are some of the things you can do to move fashion from where it is to a completely new place? This is what is meant by *serving* what you are passionate about: you are assisting it, helping it get from one place to the place where you would like to see it, thus creating an ideal for yourself. Above all, you must be completely convinced of your method and have the utmost confidence in your ideal, regardless of the thoughts and opinions of others. Mandela's passion was the people, and he served his passion by combating institutionalised racism and inequality. This was his ideal.

As mentioned at the beginning of this book, there is and always will be someone watching you. You as a young king must realise that those who share your optimism in your ideal will often look to you for inspiration. This is the second part of leadership: being an example.

Being an example is being a model of imitation. This is not to say that others will desire to be like you, but when you can give others a sense of revelation and motivation to move forward with their own ideals, you have just acted the part of a leader.

So often we expect leaders to cut this perfect exterior. We want our leaders to be great orators. We want them to demonstrate authority and never show weakness. Leadership is more of an inward display of resolve rather than an outward show of power, and many are overlooked for positions of leadership because they do not look like a leader. There are men with amazing insight and wonderful vision, but because they stuttered when they spoke, or may have made a mistake or two in the past, they were disqualified from certain positions.

We are a culture obsessed with titles. We love position and authority, but the truth is you can be in charge and not be a leader. Real leadership does not need a badge or a name tag, it does not need a seat up front or a reserved parking space; it is the knowledge of understanding your passion and purpose, and being willing to help others get to the same place of understanding.

Leadership is not always connected to position. It is possible to lead without being titled. Again, it is all about having the knowledge to understand what leading is all about. When you are in possession of this knowledge, trying to compete for a role becomes a waste of time. Too many men are busy playing a game of snakes and ladders with their careers, not caring who they step on or manipulate, seeing themselves as crabs in a barrel, as long as they get to the top. Your identity as a king gives you the confidence to know you are already at the top. Kings are not intimidated by their bosses and are not easily drawn in when it comes to office politics. A king does not scratch when nothing is itching and does not laugh when nothing is funny. Those immature pastimes are for the insecure, not for a young man of valour.

It is not possible for every man to be the CEO, the pastor, or the president, but it is possible for every man to be a leader. When you assess your life, and everything that it possesses, all of that is yours to lead.

In whichever shape or form, there are some people in your life who are waiting to grab a piece of motivation from you. You cannot lead without knowing how to serve, and it is hard to effectively serve if you do not have anything to be passionate about. Leadership is having the guts to want to make a difference, not so you can have your name in lights, but because you have the platform from which to do so. Never think you are too young (or even too old) to be a leader, for it is the right of every man to be a servant. A life without passion is a wasted one.

Many of our young kings will essentially forfeit their roles as leaders because there is nothing in their lives they care that much for. Find something that motivates you, find something you feel strongly about, and use the uniqueness of who you are to push the boat out and make a difference. The individual who lives the extraordinary life will always be singled out as an example. Live the type of life that other people will gain strength from. When you have been knocked down by a circumstance, get back up and show everyone else that the only option is to keep moving.

Live the type of life that will leave a glowing legacy. When it is all said and done, the world may not know your name; they might, but just in case they don't, let there be someone, somewhere who will say because of your life, they were able to be encouraged, they were able to be uplifted, they were able to find their passion and light up another candle from the flame of a life well lived. Do not seek to have your name on a door, do not be in pursuit of a headline, and do not live for the applause and the adoration of others. All of that will come when you make the decision to be a game changer in this world. Build your ideal; go after your passion with sincerity, hunger, and good intentions, and you will naturally lead those who believe in your vision. Do not lead from your position, but lead from your heart. Be determined rather than stubborn, stick to your guns, and live the best life that you possibly can.

Phase V

M.I.A.
(MISSING IN ARISTOCRACY)

"Is there no King in your midst?"

Micah 4.9

The beautiful, harmonious Caribbean spice island of Grenada was the birthplace of both of my parents. In 1993, my mother and father took my twin sister and me on our very first visit. The one thing I will never forget from that trip was seeing how the locals treated my father. I had never seen a man so respected. Everywhere we went, we would bump into someone he knew. The looks on their faces when they saw him was one of genuine delight and gladness. It was at that moment when I realised how popular my father was. The entire trip, I did not leave him alone. I wanted to go everywhere he went. I wanted everyone to know that this man whom everyone loved is my dad.

Most six-year-olds who had a connection with their father like I did would no doubt see him as some kind of hero. For every boy, his dad is the standard.

In my young, enthusiastic six-year-old imagination, I was convinced that pop was the king of Grenada.

In a strange way, fathers are the first image a boy sees of his own identity. All of the things his dad would tell teach and show him, that boy would try and do it the way Dad did it.

That boy would learn certain small aspects of what a man does from his father. The father would be the one to teach his son how to tie a tie, how to shine his shoes, how to use a public urinal. That boy would have paid close attention to the way his dad shaved, drove a car, spoke to strangers, even the way he cooked and fixed things around the house. His father is his guide in the journey to becoming a man. As a boy, the one thing you did not want to do was disappoint Dad. Pride and approval were the two things every boy craves from his father.

The birth of a king's son is a major occasion in the lives of monarchs. It signifies the continuation of royalty. That young boy is groomed from birth to walk in his father's footsteps. He is taught to pay close attention, as one day he will be the one to assume his father's role.

There are cases in history, however, where a boy has been given the mantle of monarch from birth. King Alfonso XIII of Spain was born on the 17th of May, 1886, and began his reign as king on that day. This was due to his father, King Alfonso XII, dying a few months before his son was born. Alfonso XIII took full control of the helm when he turned sixteen; all the while, his mother held control in his place. His mother was the one who was fulfilling both roles in his life; she was his mother and his example as a king.

This scenario is a common one today. Many young kings are travelling through adolescent life without a male example. No generation has experienced the lack of fathers more than this one. The truth is, dads are M.I.A. It is often said that when a father is absent, the mother plays both roles. This is not entirely an accurate statement; the mother may do double the work, but no one other than a man can teach a boy about the details of his manhood.

When a boy does not have his father to show him the way, his only perspective about all aspects of life comes from his mother in terms of a parental structure. Now, this is in no way an attempt to discredit the miraculous job single mothers do, but some mothers need to understand that without a male influence, that boy can never really be too sure about what is expected of him if he does not have a tangible pattern to follow.

Sometimes a mother's perspective on manhood can be accurate, powerful, and meaningful, other times it can be damaging, harmful, and detrimental. Once these negative outlooks are pressed upon a boy, he will find it hard to find his feet as a man.

The young king growing up without his father's influence has not been shown how a man deals with the issues of life. When his mother is angry, she may shout, when she is upset, she may cry, but how does this young man deal with the turbulence in his heart without a male example? He may experience feelings of confusion, not really knowing what is expected of him, and as a consequence may begin to overcompensate. The lines are blurred in his mind as to how aggressive is too aggressive, how soft is too soft, which puts his balance out of sync, and this puts his task as a man in jeopardy. His boyhood stage is not complete, those experiences of love and acceptance a boy needs from his father are not present, and this could create potentially toxic situations in his adult life.

From an early age, a boy is encouraged not to show weakness of any kind. When boys cry, they are swiftly told to stop. In their teens, it is a stigma to show any kind of emotion. This suppressed, confined emotional mentality would have these young men looking for what they crave in completely the wrong places. Gangs are attractive to young men, because if you think about it, they offer the perfect family set-up: love, loyalty, protection, togetherness. There is something powerful about validation in the life of a man, and these gangs provide that need, that craving to be wanted, that their father is responsible for filling.

We are creatures of imitation. This is especially true of young men. Young males will seek to imitate who they *identify* with, whether that person is Dad, big brother, Granddad, Pastor, an athlete, a celebrity, whoever. The point is they will find someone to emulate. Whatever the reason for finding identification from a young man in these individuals, it is usually down to the type of upbringing he has experienced. Whatever he has witnessed or has been exposed to in his learning and development years will most likely manifest itself in some way, shape, or form once he reaches the stage of accountability. The problem we are having from a sociological perspective is we have damaged men who had illegitimate examples as boys. If nothing has been done to fix the broken areas in the lives of men, a continuous cycle of false representation and illegal identities will filter through to their sons. Without anything being done, how is a boy supposed to act different if he consistently witnessed his example putting his hands on his mother? Without anything being done, how do you convince a man to marry when his example never thought it was necessary? Without anything being done, how do you instil upstanding values and morals when his example is on television, promoting a lifestyle of extreme opulence, bad language, and disrespecting women?

Far be it from me to offer any kind of solution or counsel on this subject, for each case is a different one, but if I could speak to the young king who is currently roaming through life without his father, if I could speak to a single mother, or even the father who is apart from his son, this is what I probably would say.

To the King without a Father

The following is what I would say if you ever get to the stage where you absolutely want to.

First things first. Whatever the reason your dad may not be present in your life, none of it is your fault. His decisions are not a reflection on you. You may be feeling a sense of anger and bitterness towards him, which is natural, but for your own sake, you cannot continue to endorse those feelings. Before you can think about forgiving him, forgive yourself. Forgive yourself for even thinking that somehow, because you never had a father in your life, that you are this broken, indifferent shambles of a person. I have learnt that all things we go through are lessons, and somewhere, somehow, you have to look for the lesson in every situation. Your lesson from this could be about fatherhood; take it seriously. When your time comes to raise a child, learn from your experiences and let them aid you into becoming a good father to your children.

It is important that you find and develop a healthy relationship with a man, if it is not your dad. Not just any man, but a trusting, loving individual you know can deposit wisdom and a sense of self-worth into your soul. It can be someone from your church, a teacher or lecturer from school, an uncle or an older cousin: someone who can mentor you through the difficult stages of your life.

Understand that your life is important; your identity is set before you. If you are currently growing up without your father present, it bears no significance to who you are. In cases like yours, you are special to God.

"When my father and mother forsake me, then the Lord will take care of me."

Psalm 27:10

Acknowledge your feelings and be honest about them. This could cause you pain that you do not want to deal with, but it is essential for healing (if you see this as a broken area in your life) to begin. Do not deny your hurt. Ignoring your pain can create a confinement in your mind that could take years to break free from.

If you ever get into a situation in the future where you see your father again, it is important you tell him exactly how you feel. This is the tough part, and this is where you may need the support of your mother if you do not feel entirely comfortable confronting him. This is an important step to take if you still have feelings of resentment. You must release them in the most positive way. Confrontation is one of the best ways of healing the matters of the heart. Be brave about it if you choose to go down that road with your father. If you do not want to confront him face to face but would still like to tell him how you feel, write him a letter. Be transparent in your approach, tell him how you felt about him not being available when you needed him, tell him what you thought about him (choose your words carefully here), and you would be amazed at the release you will feel at expressing your emotions to him, even if it is on paper. Hold your head up; refuse to tell yourself stories of what could have been if your father was around. Your future is depending on you. Remember: do, only if you want to.

To the Mother Raising a King

Your role is a unique and special one in the life of your son. Boys without a father present can sometimes have this wonderful connection with their mothers when they see that you are one of the consistencies in his life. Do understand that while you can give him everything he needs, he is still seeking stability and togetherness from a masculine mindset. This should have no bearing on the job that you have done in his life. Your son can be a well-rounded, intelligent individual under your care, and regardless of how he feels about his father, present or not, he needs to be shown the ropes according to his manhood.

He needs your prayers, your support, and your trust more than he needs constant badgering and control. No son would ever fall off the wagon if the words "I am his mother and I know what's best for him" were true. It is important to attempt to lay the foundations of his manhood early by first recognising what they are. Show him that he can be trusted. Let him pick out his own clothes; let him run to the store and buy the carrots for dinner even if you don't need them. If you can match that with reminding him about his self-worth, teaching him how to pray, and recognising his importance to you and to himself, he will begin to develop responsibility and independence; which means in the moments he is away from you and surrounded by those who can influence him, he stands a better chance of making good decisions.

Encourage him to get involved in things where he can be introduced to other men you know who can mentor him. You more than anyone can lead him to someone you know who will take your son under his wing without any ulterior motive.

Do use wisdom in what you say to your son about his father, if he ever asks about him. Anything you say in terms of an insult could make your son think he is the reason for those feelings. Be honest, but always give him reassurance about who he is as a young man.

The blame game is a fruitless exercise. Getting into the arena about the dynamics between you and your son's father is a discussion for another time. It is certainly not for the ears of your son. What has to be dealt with is the reality of the situation, and the reality is your son must know what it is like to experience the love from a father. Never close the door on any potential relationship that may occur between your son and his dad, and as you keep that door open, encourage your son the best you can that he can walk through that door, if he wants to.

To the Mentor

When it comes to the saying "It takes a village to raise a child," you are the village they are talking about.

Kings inspire other kings. It is the role of the men of our communities to be a beacon of light to these fatherless kings. Even though these boys are not your biological sons, they still belong to you. There is a duty not just to them, not just to their mothers, not just to yourself, but a duty on a global scale to steer these young men from a life of destruction to a life of destiny. I make no apologies by saying if we can save our young men, we can save the world at large.

We need other men who will have a heart for these boys. The fatherless sons of our world are seeking someone who will let them know how proud they are of them, someone who can be a role model, and someone who can be honest with them and share their stories in an attempt to inspire self-worth.

If the mentors are going to be anything to these young men, be consistent. Above everything else.

Have no reason to be in his life other than the desire to see him succeed, not because it might make you look good, and certainly do not use him as an avenue to get to his mother.

To King Sr

King Jr needs you, however you feel about it. There is a reality to be thought of here. What we are faced with is your son potentially stumbling his way through life because he does not have anyone to switch the lights on for him.

Situations as this one can originate from a vast number of factors. As mentioned before, we are naturally people of habit; anything we see done, we will probably imitate as long as it is within our capacity to do so. Many fathers are repeating to their sons what was done to them. It is this cycle of issues that are never dealt with coming back to manifest itself in the mind of our offspring.

There is no such thing as too late to make amends. It does not matter how old your son might be, the one thing you do not want to do is leave this earth without ever at the very least acknowledging him as your son.

The onus should not be on him to make the first move of communication if one is to be established. If he chooses to, then that is different, but he should not have to be forced into speaking to you.

Avoid thoughts of *Well, he doesn't want to speak to me anyway.* Ignore such consideration, and understand he may have a range of feelings and emotions he is trying to deal with, and it can sometimes manifest itself into aggression.

If it is your desire to make a reconnection with your son, the only thing there is to say is, go for it. If your son is relatively young, share something with him that you love. Pick him up from school, take the day off from work, and share an activity with him. He will remember all those small things you did with him, and that would add to his self-esteem.

If your son is a grown man, share a story with him, be honest and open in front of him, tell him why you thought it was important to want to grow a relationship with him again.

Do not allow guilt to swallow you alive. Guilt could hold you back from wanting to be in your son's life. Guilt could make all the excuses under the sun for you, but do not allow it to. Realise that you are important to someone, whether it seems like it or not, someone needs you. Self-condemnation will do nothing but keep you bound.

Whatever the relationship between you and your son's mother, whether stable or not, that is something that must be laid aside for the sake and sanity of your son. He may be able to come to terms with his parents not being together, but at the end of the day, he will still grow into a man, and he needs the foundation only a father can give in order to live a fulfilled and prosperous life.

Interlude

THE ROYAL COMMANDMENTS

- *Thou shall never forget God and at all times be accountable to Him.*

- *Thou shall seek wisdom and keep the company of those smarter than himself.*

- *Thou shall be himself at all times and must remain mindful that false representation is illegal.*

- *Thou shall discover what he is good at and pursue it passionately.*

- *Thou shall only speak that which is positive and at no time utter negatives over himself or anyone else.*

- *Thou shall always be mindful of his worth and shall never forget it.*

- *Thou shall never expect a woman to play the role of wife before he makes her one.*

- *Thou shall remain humble. At no time shall he feel the need to show off, keep up appearance, or perform for applause.*

- *Thou shall move with authority, walk with head held high, and maintain excellence.*

- *Thou shall remember to keep his crown on at all times.*

Phase VI

BOY MEETS WORLD

"When a man starts out to build a world, he
starts first with himself."

Langston Hughes

T he public spotlight for a king is a glaring one. Everything, down to the smallest detail, is monitored. The truth is, everyone has a moral obligation when it comes to the matters of behaviour and conduct, but for a king, those obligations are all the more forceful.

There is an enormous and sometimes unfair expectation for a king to appear blameless. To maintain the trust of the people, there cannot be any glaring faults found in his persona. If any is found, his position is not directly threatened; he will still be king regardless, but what he will lose is respect, power, and status, and it is the loss of those things that can ultimately lose him his position.

A king is expected to wear a certain type of clothing, he is expected to talk a certain way, and his mannerisms are expected to be of a certain kind. Although this sounds forced and unnecessary, it is actually to signal that he is different from everyone else. It is all to symbolise his role as a king and to make clear that he is not supposed to be like everyone else.

I say this to show that your behaviour and conduct is important. Today's kings must hold on to a standard to show the world that they are indeed different from the rest.

Kings are gentlemen. Kings are well mannered and in control of themselves at all times. Kings are chivalrous; they pay attention to etiquette and are always mindful of others.

It is essential to show royal conduct in a world where there isn't any. We are living in a time where lawlessness, immorality, and selfishness fill the hearts of men everywhere. Young men are forever stereotyped and written off due to their behaviour.

Your role as a king is to restore grace, dignity, and decency in this world. Let's face it; the whole "thug" image is played out. To be well put together in appearance and personality is no longer just reserved for the distinguished gentleman who wears suits on his days off and carries a briefcase, but it is expected of all men regardless of age, ethnicity, or background.

Chivalry isn't dead, it just got lost amongst the boring macho, chauvinistic nature that so many young men try to imitate. A king is a well-rounded individual. He is not predictable, but he is always consistent. A king is in touch with current affairs and his surroundings. He understands that class is alluring and manners are attractive. Nothing is out of his control as he remains firmly on top of his responsibilities. Let's explore some of the areas of conduct that is expected of a young king growing up in today's world.

Appearance

I believe C. Joybell C said it best: "A clown on a throne is still a clown. A king in rags is still a king."

In the grand scheme of things, your clothes are not that important. They are not an indication of what is truly important about a person. However, they play a big part of your personage. We live in a world of first impressions. Jobs are nowadays lost not by what the interviewee said, but what the interviewer saw. Your attire doesn't have to be complicated, but there are some guidelines to follow.

All young kings must own a suit. It doesn't have to be expensive, but it must fit well. A dark coloured suit with a contrasting tie and a fitted white shirt won't have you looking out of place in any setting. If you are only going to have one suit, make it a solid black one. A black suit signifies power and class. A black suit is often reserved for more formal occasions, but for work, church, or graduation, you cannot go wrong with a navy or charcoal grey colour. A pinstripe suit is a more stylish, relaxed option. Keep your suit buttoned while standing, and feel free to loosen it while sitting. Never do up all the buttons on your suit, but always leave the last one unbuttoned. If your suit has two buttons, button the top only. If your suit has three buttons, do up the first two, but the rule is to always leave the bottom button undone.

The top button on your shirt must be done up at all times if you have a tie on. If you wish to undo the top button of your shirt for comfort, remove the tie completely. Keep your formal accessories simple and classic. Items such as neckties, cufflinks, and pocket squares have to be worn with confidence. Be bold, but do not be garish. Cartoon ties or ties with your favourite sports teams' logo on it are a no-no. Do not ask me why, they just are.

If your main source of ability to tell the time comes from your cell phone, it is time to buy a watch. I understand the technological advances that phones have made in the last fifteen years, but a smart wristwatch is, and will always be, the gentleman's choice of timekeeping. Your shoes must remain scuff free and polished. In essence, a pair of black oxfords would compliment any suit, but if you want to be stylish, save them for your black suit only. A pair of brown brogues would instantly add a touch of character to a navy or a grey suit. Compliment your brown shoes with a brown belt. Loafers provide a more elegant touch. They are usually reserved for tuxedos, but you can wear a tasselled or plain pair comfortably these days without appearing dated. If you are going to travel the route of coloured socks, remember one thing: socks are supposed to match your trousers, *not* your shoes, according to popular belief.

When it comes to your casual or less formal wear, again, wear what you feel most comfortable in. Resist the urge to follow fashion. There is nothing less appealing than a young man splashed head to toe in designer labels for everyone to see. There is power in subtlety; be discreet in your fashion choices. 'Look at me' clothing is reserved for attention seekers, not kings. Keep your sneakers clean and your jeans fitted. If your trousers or jeans have loops, use them; wear a belt.

It has to be stressed, young men: trousers above the waist. Please, please, please. Understand that trend came from the prison where inmates would wear their trousers below their waist as a sign for others that they are available for sex. It is not the kind of message your identity will have you deliver.

If you wish to wear a fragrance, the golden rule is less is more. It is offensive to everyone around you when you spray liberally. Depending on your scent's concentration, two sprays behind each ear will be enough. Resist the urge to re-apply. After some time, you nose will become immune to your scent, but believe me when I say everyone will still be able to detect a smell even if you don't.

Make it a routine to visit the barbershop a couple of times a month. Stay sharp and presentable where your hair is concerned. Remain well groomed. Keep your teeth clean, your breath fresh, your nails short, and your skin looking vibrant.

In my opinion, there are many fashion faux pas that are outdated. To me, it is perfectly acceptable for a man to wear a hat for any occasion, even to wear sunglasses indoors. It is about maintaining what works for you.

Simplicity is golden. Classic beats trends. Never appear like you are trying too hard to be fashionable when it comes to your sartorial choices. Above all, be you.

Speech

Life and death is in the power of the tongue. A king's mouth is not the law, but he carries the law in his mouth. What you say carries far more weight and significance than you think.

Let's start by saying this: there is nothing wrong with domesticated language (slang). It is important, however, not to overdo it. There are ways of remaining current without following a trend. I'm not saying it is a must to speak the Queen's English and to properly annunciate every word, regional accents won't allow that, but a professional setting will require a more learned manner of speech. Remember who you are speaking to at all times. Addressing your superior or your parents is not the same as addressing your peers. If you are interacting with strangers, always refer to an older gentleman as "sir" and an older lady as "madam" or "ma'am."

Request nothing without saying please, and receive nothing without saying thank you. These are simple seeds sown in the soil of success. Remember to use them at all times.

Foul language is a no-go area. If you have a habit of using offensive speech, do your best to try and rid yourself from it. It can come back to haunt you if it slips out at an inappropriate time.

Never speak ill of anyone, regardless of the situation. Throwing insults around says more about you than it does about them.

You live in the real world, not the playground, so the words "Did you hear ..." should never be a part of your vocabulary. Gossip is poisonous. Never indulge in it, and by all accounts never start a rumour about anything or anyone.

Never talk for the sake of talking. It is okay not to have anything to say. Intelligence knows you do not always have to say something or always have an opinion.

Speak positive of yourself and others. Lift someone up with encouraging words, say a prayer for someone who may be having a tough time, and remember the ancient rule: think before you speak.

Social Decorum

Your social life is important. It is healthy to maintain interests with other people. How you are viewed in public is up to you.

There are expectations of a king to fulfil a role when he is invited to a gathering. Never ignore an invitation. Accept with grace if you wish to go; decline with respect if you do not. If the occasion happens to be a celebration (i.e., wedding, birthday party, or anniversary) always bring a gift. The more formal the occasion, the more important it is to be on time. If the occasion is not so formal (i.e., house party, barbeque) be mindful of the time asked of the host to arrive and be respectful of it.

Be in control of yourself at all times. Monitor your alcohol consumption if you wish to have a drink (strictly for those over eighteen). Drunkard behaviour is not acceptable. Do not be the loudest person in the room. Your demeanour will draw people to you, so there is no need to want to be the life and soul of the party. Always thank the host for the invitation when leaving.

Social media is a great way to network. It can be a useful tool to stay in touch with distant relatives and friends. It can, like most things, become a detriment if used incorrectly. Be mindful of what you make public; as a king, what you say can and will be used against you. Never address a problem publicly, and at no time appear inappropriate or indecent.

When travelling on public transport, always give up your seat for someone who appears less able to stand. Allow ladies to board a bus or a train first, and keep your feet off the seat. If you are listening to music through headphones, be considerate. Keep the volume at a comfortable level for yourself and those around you.

When in a setting such as a formal dinner at a restaurant, remember not to talk with your mouth full and keep the volume down on your conversation. If your food is not to the standard you wanted, politely mention it to the waiter or waitress. If you are ordering wine, do not pretend to be a connoisseur when the most Italian beverage you have ever tried is a sambucca. Go with red wine if you are ordering red meat or anything spicy; go with white wine for foods such as fish and chicken. Ask the waiter or waitress for a recommendation on which wine to choose. Always hold a wine glass by the stem. Do not eat or drink anything you do not like in an attempt to impress whoever you are dining with. Keep your cell phone off the table; if it does happen to ring, do not answer it. If it rings several times, excuse yourself and take the call quickly, as it might be an emergency.

If in the presence of a lady, a gentleman always pays. It may seem like an old fashioned concept, but it remains a staple of etiquette for a man. If she insists on paying, politely refuse and tell her you will split it with her next time.

Always leave a tip. Either for your waiter, your barber, or anyone who has served you.

As a king, understand that morals and integrity far outweigh street credentials and a reputation. Aim for excellence in everything you do.

Mannerisms

Years ago, my primary school teacher told me, "Manners are free." It is customary for kings to be well mannered and polite at all times. His customs and standards are important when in public display.

When in conversation, pay attention and listen intently. Do not interrupt and only speak when the other person has finished talking. Look a person in the eye when in a discussion, but do not glare at them.

Only give your opinion if asked for it; never volunteer your views. If you have to excuse yourself from the conversation, be apologetic, and ensure the other person you will finish your discussion another time.

Your demeanour ought to be the same regardless of your company. From the president to the homeless, address others the way you would wish to be addressed.

We live in a dog-eat-dog world, and a timid individual is another man's pushover. Be affable and authoritative at the same time. Say what you mean, and mean what you say. Be considerate of the feelings of others, but do not beat around the bush either. If you feel that you have been disrespected in any way, do not make a big deal about it, but do not tolerate it either. Go to the person and seek a resolution. If the shoe happens to be on the other foot, it is important that you listen and apologise, and explain that you meant no harm. Do not make an excuse for any poor behaviour.

Never walk with your head facing the ground. Of course, look where you are going, but keep your head held high. Pay attention to your posture, sit upright, and stand straight. Not only are you demonstrating professionalism, but you are doing your back a world of good too. No slouching unless you are in the comfort of your own home. Be mindful of your body language. Crossed arms signal nervousness and insecurity; the only times your arms should be crossed is if you are cold. Try not to fidget. You do not want to appear nervous for no reason; maintain your cool. Most importantly, smile. It is an action that is understood by any person on the planet. It brings encouragement to those who need it and a mutual understanding when words fail.

Health and Fitness

Your body is your temple.

If you desire to live a full, long life, you must look after yourself. Let's first address diet. Eating what you want, when you want is not the wisest choice to make. Your body will not forgive you for it in the future. Eating this way can lead to many complications in later life. When it comes to food, it does not have to be complicated. A balanced diet is a variation of foods from each food group (the food groups being fruit and vegetables, milk and dairy foods, sugars, meat and fish, and starchy foods such as potatoes and rice). Do not overdo each individual group, but an even spread of foods from each group, coupled with plenty of water, will be fine. As much as you can, avoid processed foods and beverages loaded with sugar and caffeine. Our busy lives sometimes rely on something quick and in a hurry, as we don't have time to sit and eat an entire meal, and fast food is perfect for that scenario. Make your consumption of fast food as rare as possible, as it has an alarmingly high fat and sugar count that is no good for your heart.

It is recommended that you do at least thirty minutes of physical exercise a day. As much as your physical body needs to be in shape, so does your heart. If you have difficulty with exercise, or find it hard to get motivated, start small. Get off the bus a few stops earlier and walk the rest of the way. There are plenty of calisthenic exercises you can do in the comfort of your bedroom, such as star jumps, squats, and pushups. Getting in shape and remaining that way takes time and discipline. Stick to it, and you will in time reap the benefits of being in optimum health.

Rest is a vital part of remaining healthy. Getting up to eight hours of sleep a night has many benefits. Improved memory, sharper attention, lowered stress, and even weight loss are all impacted for the better by sleep. It can also improve your general sense of happiness, attitude, and mental state.

You are no good to anyone in sickness. Be mindful of your health, and make the steps to improve if you feel you are lacking.

Attitudes towards Work

Work is not the direct correlation to a job we think it is. Just because someone does not have a job does not mean they cannot work.

A king is someone who is no stranger to working. He is not opposed to work and finds a sense of achievement whenever he is put to work.

Scripture says, "He who has a slack hand becomes poor, but the hand of the diligent makes rich." In other words, lazy men never prosper.

If you are not currently in employment, there is still work for you to do. Start with the simple things. Make it your duty to take out the garbage every week, keep your bedroom clean, start by making small differences in your home. This will build up your tolerance and attitude towards working.

When it comes to employment, always do your best in whatever arena of vocation you do. The two golden rules when at work are simply to work hard and be on time.

Do not fall into the trap of only doing the minimum. Doing just enough of what is required of you will not get you fired, but it will not get you noticed either. Kings never fly under the radar. Your lifestyle should be one that cannot help but make people recognise you. Even if you wanted to keep a low profile, there is someone at work watching you and paying attention to the work that you do. Go above and beyond (within reason). Always do more than what is expected, but be careful not to be excessive; unless you are the boss, adhere to the guidelines of your position.

Unless you are legitimately unwell, do not call in sick. Attendance is important. If you happen to be working on a day when there is an event you wish to attend, speak to your supervisor or ask a colleague to swap a shift; if neither option is viable, use a day of holiday. Do not lie when it is not necessary. Practicing your "sick voice" in the mirror in an attempt to fool your manager is not dignified. You have a responsibility at your place of employment to show up, and you don't want to jeopardise your position when there are countless of people who are out of work who will take your place in a heartbeat.

Do not let your work consume you. Understand that all work and no play makes for a boring individual. Find the correct balance between work and leisure and maintain it. Work hard, but make time for your loved ones.

Managing Finances

Having worked in the bank for over twenty years, my mother taught me some valuable lessons when it came to managing money. One of the things she taught me from a very early age was simply to "spend a little, save a little." She explained to me that there was nothing wrong with enjoying money, as long as my saving matched my spending.

It is important to monitor your spending habits; it takes discipline to be a good steward of your own money. Keep a log of how much you spend and what you buy. Sometimes, to have more just means to spend less. Debt can follow you for a long time unless you learn to deal with it. If you do have debts, make sure you set up a monthly repayment plan so you are not leaving yourself short, and stick to it until you are completely debt free.

Arranging a savings plan is a good way to keep a little extra something tucked away for a rainy day. It doesn't have to be a lot of money, but a consistent amount each week or month can quickly add up to a sizable amount. A good way to save money is the "day and pounds" method, where according to what number of day it is in the year, you will save the same amount in pounds. For example, on the first day of the year you will put aside one pound, on the second, two pounds, the third, three pounds, all the way until the 365th day of the year. If you stick to it, you will be amazed at how much money you are able to save in a year. I'll let you do the maths on how much exactly.

Spend for the right reasons. I know this might sound strange, but you would be amazed at the amount of people who will spend money they do not really have, to buy things they do not really need, to impress people they do not really like. There is a temptation, especially amongst many young people, to buy things to keep up appearances. Make smart choices when it comes to spending. Don't stretch yourself just to maintain an image.

We all at times fall into difficult positions where we need an amount of money we do not have. If you ask to borrow money, make paying the person back a priority, assess how you got yourself into financial trouble in the first place, and make the steps to ensure you will not have to borrow from anyone again.

If someone asks you to borrow money, use your own discretion. It is not a good idea to give if it means it will leave you stretched, even if your intentions are good. Only give if you can do without. If you cannot do without, do not give. If you can afford to lose it, you can afford to not ask for it back. I know that sounds strange, but you do not want to get into a position where you are constantly asking for your money. This scenario can sour relationships and damage trust.

Learn to be the kind of man you want your son to be and the type of man you wish your daughter to bring home. Unfortunately, some people will judge you by your cover; if so, you may as well give them something to look at. Straighten your tie, flash a smile, and build your kingdom.

Phase VII

IN SEARCH OF CORETTA

"Who, being loved, is poor?"

Oscar Wilde

(Disclaimer: The content of this chapter is for the mature of mind only. Reader discretion is advised. Enjoy!)

Men do not show emotion. Men are not to appear sensitive and are not to display any type of behaviour that can be interpreted as "soft." Men are to put money before women at all times, regardless of the situation, and are certainly not in any way, shape, or form to trust a person of the opposite sex.

If you were to buy into the attitude by men towards women these days, you would probably share the same ideals as these.

Somewhere, somehow, adolescent men have developed this harsh, rugged, and hoarse approach towards the idea of relationships, and women in general.

There is a "hit and quit" mentality that surrounds our young men. Sex has become the goal, and anything else is out of bounds. Egos have been bruised and hearts have been broken, and as a consequence, both young men and women would at times rather experience the physical pleasure of a relationship without any kind of emotion attached. Interaction with the opposite sex for young men has become nothing more than a numbers game. Bragging rights to our peers is the trophy in the conquest of how many notches we can get on the bedpost.

Trust is lost, and disrespect is found. Some young men are quick to refer to women as female dogs, even when they have a sister and a mother at home.

There are many valid points as to where exactly these values come from towards women. One thing is for sure, however; love in my generation has long drifted from the Romeo and Juliet mantle and is somewhere on the side of the road, in the rain, broken and battered, waiting for help.

In my honest and transparent opinion, there is nothing God has created on this earth more beautiful than the woman. The Bible refers to the woman as the "weaker vessel," only in comparison generally to a man's physical strength, but this also reminds me of the allure and delicacy of her femininity. She is to be handled with care, she is not to be played with, and she is to be protected.

For centuries, women have been mistreated. They have been seen as objects for entertainment, pleasure, and financial gain. From the days of slavery, when they were repeatedly raped or forced to nurse children they did not give birth to, to being mutilated as young girls in an attempt to control their sexuality. To being sold into the sex trade and made to operate as robots, severely damaging their self-esteem and self-worth, along with the physical and physiological infliction it bestows upon them, to being handled like punch bags by husbands, brothers, and fathers alike.

I make no apology for the vivid and graphic imagery I may be painting in your mind here, but I see men as the underlying, deep-rooted common denominator for a lot of the pain some women have to experience, all because men have failed to safeguard her, but to use and abuse her is seen as the ultimate display of power for some men.

It is time for men to act responsibly. Many of the negative attitudes adopted by women are through her dealings with the opposite sex. She has developed the same heart that C. S. Lewis described when it is locked away in a box; the box being the best method of protection, it will never get hurt, but while locked away, never seeing light or experiencing air, it becomes unbreakable and impenetrable, unable to feel love, or anything, for that matter.

Can we blame some women for their harsh interiors? Can we blame some for their lack of trust in men?

Women, who are now void of emotion, passion, and love, are changing the game. They are beginning to treat many good, honest men the way they have been treated in the past. Today, it is some women who are using men for entertainment and pleasure; today, there are women who are physically and mentally abusing the husbands, brothers, and fathers in their lives.

What we are now left with, after generations of mismanagement, after centuries of mistreating one another, is a formation of young men and young women who do not trust each other, who are struggling to give and receive love, all due to the overwhelming and crushing fear of experiencing love-related pain of the heart.

I will say it again; it is time for men to act responsibly. Our attitudes towards women have to change. We must think about protecting our women. Not because we want them to fall in love with us, not because we want to be seen as the knight in shining armour, but simply because it is our duty to do so.

To protect her isn't to shield her away from the dangers of the world, but it is simply to allow her to live in the freedom to be herself. It is the natural instinct for her to *want* to nurture, to *want* to love, to *want* to feel beautiful, but we are handicapping her of that right.

As a king, you protect. That is as simplistic as I can put it. You protect your home, you protect your name, and you protect your women. Your wife, your mother, your sister, your niece, your granddaughter, your aunts, even the women who are not directly related to you, you protect and defend them at any cost.

It is important for the dynamic of our culture and our communities that we have healthy relationships between young men and young women, and that we also have healthy examples of relationships between men and women of another generation. By a "healthy relationship," I mean a suitable and appropriate interaction between opposite sexes in the context of friendship, dating, and marriage.

We must have a definitive description of love and have the correct picture of it also. We can no longer continue to misinterpret it and treat like the step-child of ambiguity.

Possibly the most beautiful and precise definition of love is found in scripture:

"Love suffers long and it is kind, love does not envy, love does not parade itself, is not puffed up, does not behave rudely, does not seek its own, is not provoked, thinks no evil, does not rejoice in iniquity, but rejoices in the truth, bears all things, believes all things, hopes all things, endures all things."

1 Corinthians 13:4–7

If you have ever been to a church wedding, this verse will most likely be quoted. Although not specifically referring to love between two people, the writer artistically explains the characteristics of love. You can translate it to fit platonic love and the love between a mother and her child. It is a wonderful image of sacrifice and selflessness. Love by this definition is gloriously innocent and delightfully optimistic.

In order to want to experience love and in turn give, there must be vulnerability. This is the area that many people struggle with. When there is love in action, it does not think about self, it seeks to gratify, and it does all of this willingly. By way of illustration, love is taking your own heart and placing it in the hands of someone else, with the hope they will look after it and not mistreat it.

It is risky, and it appears dangerous, but those are natural thoughts that come with being vulnerable. True love cannot exist if an emotional wall is built; you have to be willing to let the other person see all of you and allow them to choose to accept what they see, and vice versa.

While it is important to be vulnerable, it is probably even more important not to be reckless. There is nothing wrong with desiring to want to be in love, but there is when you are dangling your heart from the end of a fishing rod and sitting at the side of the sea. As with everything, patience is a virtue, but it is dangerous to you, and damaging to your self-esteem, when you give your heart to the first person who shows signs of interest.

Love, in itself, is a wonderful journey, but a journey nonetheless. If you ask me if I believe in love at first sight, my thoughts would be incredibly pessimistic towards it. That is not to say I absolutely reject the idea. This journey is an exciting one in the lives of many young people. Some call it "courtship," others call it "dating," and there are differences between the two.

Courting is a specific and spiritual type of what we know as dating. It is the relationship between a man and a woman who seek whether it is in the will of God for the two to marry. Courting is the choice to abstain from the physical (you know what I mean) and to invest more time into exploring other aspects of the relationship. Each couple's version of courtship (should they choose one) is different.

The main difference between dating and courtship is dating is the ideology of seeking someone who will make us happy. Courting is discerning the will of God for direction when considering who to spend forever with.

Traditionally, courtship is a non-complicated agreement. If two have agreed to enter this arena of a relationship, then they are both aware that they have marriage as a goal in mind. Dating, although not always the case, doesn't have this particular view. Some people who date will "see how things go," and though a couple may be very much in love and committed to each other, marriage is never a possibility, where with a couple who are courting, marriage is the only possibility.

Courtship can sometimes involve both families from the jump, in an attempt to establish very early what the intentions are. Again, not generally, but some couples who date can sometimes take years to introduce their significant other to their families. Yes, there are different circumstances in every scenario, but a couple who are courting will most of the time involve someone who they can trust so that person can offer wise counsel and advice when making such an important, and potentially life-changing, decision.

The "rules" surrounding dating and courting seem to be a lot more relaxed now than they have ever been. This does not mean the standard of what is required of you should follow suit.

In my opinion, your ideals towards a relationship should always be one that has marriage involved; this does not mean you need to verbalise this immediately. Your dealings with a young lady should not be for social appearances, or just because you are bored; if this is your intention, then remain single. It does not make sense wasting her time when her intentions could be different.

Every now and again, a young man will see a pretty lady who makes his heart race, his palms sweaty, and his cheeks flushed; believe me when I say young men get love struck. I have been there, and when it is someone they really like, they get it bad. She becomes all he thinks about, and it can even get to the extreme of loss of appetite and lack of sleep.

This is common among young men. I always encourage young men to do something about these feelings before it turns into an obsession, and by do something about it, I mean go and talk to her.

If she is in the same social circle as you (in the same classes, attends the same church, etc.), the opportunities you will get to talk to her will be more frequent.

If she is someone you do not see often, there is no shame in asking about her. Speak to those who know her better and make your enquiries, but never get someone to ask her out on your behalf. There is being shy, and there is being timid, and nine times out of ten it will be interpreted as the latter, and it will not sit well with her.

Be her friend first, always. Get to know her in that capacity. Most strong relationships begin with strong friendships.

Start at the beginning, say hello. Be confident in your approach. Remember, it is not a marriage proposal, you are just saying hi. Avoid corny pick-up lines and cheesy sayings. Introduce yourself, explain that you see her around from time to time, and instead of doing an awkward smile every now and again, you thought it would be better to say hello properly. Ask her how she is doing; if you share a common interest, like a college class, ask her how she is finding it. Keep your conversation brief, and recognise when it is time to excuse yourself. Be charming without making it look routine, and be bold without being cocky. When saying your good-byes, compliment her, something along the lines of "Oh, and by the way, I love your shoes." Smile, be direct with your eye contact, but do not stare at her. You do not need to do any more than that. Remember, you are not trying to be the man of her dreams at her first sight of you; you are just simply breaking the ice. Now that it is broken, allow any conversation between the two of you to happen naturally. You have already had to manufacture the hello; you do not need to manufacture anything else. Even if you feel your first interaction did not go as well as you had planned, do not worry. If she turns out to be worth your time, she would appreciate the effort you have made.

Conversation is a lost art. Today, we communicate via text message. Face to face dialogue is rare. I would encourage you to break the mould. There is nothing wrong with sending her a text every now and again, but if you have something important to say, reserve it until you see her. Too much gets lost in translation through messaging. Use a text for what it was intended to be used for: to say something quick and short that does not require a phone call. If you want to hold a conversation with her, man up and call her. She likes initiative; do not be afraid to show some.

Young women today are self-reliant. Many of them have their own cars and their own money, and they do not need a man to do anything for them, but they would still like to be courted. She wants to be asked out, and she wants to be pursued. She is aware of her value and wants you to make an effort. She will not make it easy for you, and neither should she; she is fully aware nothing good comes easy. Never make the mistake of thinking this type of woman has her standards too high; she just wants to know if you can match the standard she has set for herself. She is not stuck up, but she wants you to step up.

A woman is subtle. She is extremely tactful, very observant, and remarkably perceptive. She will very rarely come out and tell you how she feels about you, but she will use inconspicuous and discreet gestures to let you know she is interested. She will leave the door ajar and wait for you to push it wide open. Do not be the guy who cannot read between the lines. After a while, she will get tired of spending hours on the phone with you for no reason; she will get tired of explaining how she loves to eat out at restaurants and how much she loves amusement parks. Stop wondering why she is always playing with her hair when the two of you are together, why she stares at you when you are talking, and why she delicately invades your personal space every now and again. If she does these things and all of a sudden stops, she has just run out of patience and won't wait for you to figure it out.

Always be clear and precise about your intentions. Communicate to her clearly, and leave no room for confusion.

Getting to know someone is one of the more picturesque roads in the journey of life. There is a great sense of companionship when sharing things about yourself. However, take your time when getting to know someone. Be slow to reveal things about yourself, build up your tolerance for trust in that person first before sharing intimate details of your life with them.

Even though she is smart and can think for herself, she likes it when you take the lead. She does not like the question, "Well, what do you want to do?" She appreciates the time you take for thinking of something for the two of you to do. Let me stress, "Come to my house" is no longer acceptable. Be creative, and believe me, money is no excuse. Sometimes, the best dates are the ones that cost you nothing. Go to the park and bring a fruit basket, find an open air concert; there are plenty of things for you to do other than going to a restaurant and catching a movie after. Sometimes, she just wants to be in your company; other times, she wants to share an activity with you. Do not neglect one for the other.

Years ago, it was slightly taboo for young people to interact in the ways I have just mentioned; I am referring to a time when pre-marital relations were not so normal. Young people were chaperoned then; now there is a lot more freedom. The reason I bring this point up is because it was generally seen then that if young people were anywhere by themselves, they are up to no good. I may as well be frank: it was generally seen that if young people were anywhere by themselves, they were having sex. Let me first be clear about this as to avoid confusion; I believe that sex should be strictly within the covenant of marriage. Years ago, it seemed for an unmarried woman to be pregnant was the worst possible thing she could do. Some people still feel this strongly about this subject. Many believe that sex should only be between married couples, because the worst outcome outside of marriage would be a baby born out of wedlock. They will go on to argue about statistics of one-parent families should the two unmarried parents separate; they will mention the chances that child will grow up to be a disruptive member of society. The parents would be branded promiscuous, sinful fornicators, and both would be frowned upon.

I want to argue that although I agree with sex being only between a married couple, it may (or may not) surprise you that I do not support it for these reasons.

Sex is the pinnacle of closeness between a married couple. It is more than just physical pleasure, but you open yourself up emotionally, physically, psychologically, and mentally. It brings a sense of ownership to each other. It serves as a tying of souls that draw two people together. Within the confines of marriage, this is the perfect scenario. It is where you want to be with someone you are committed to. We do not live in a perfect world, and the reality is, intercourse becomes a more complicated subject when performed outside the union of marriage. There could be the emotional and psychological problem of opening yourself up and exposing the innermost intimate part of you to someone who has no interest of showing any kind of commitment. This in itself causes a problem, where the feeling of ownership could make you or the other person possessive when they have no right to be. There is also the physical problems it brings. Sexually transmitted diseases are passed around, and unprotected sex opens you up to a new world of danger for you and anyone you make the decision to sleep with next. Now these things are not bound to happen to everyone who performs intercourse without being married, but where sex is concerned, married or not, take it seriously. I would encourage you not to play too close to the edge of the cliff. Things get dangerous when not treated soberly.

Many young men I have had this discussion with say to me, "Well, how would I know I will enjoy intercourse with my future wife if I do not sleep with her before I marry her? What if I do not enjoy it?" I have even heard men say in reference to pre-marital relations, "Would you not buy a car unless you test-drove it first?"

First of all, she is a woman, not a motor vehicle. Sex ought to be the apex of intimacy between the wedded, but in the time together before you are married, spend time building a closeness with her, and over time you will be so romantically involved with each other that when you are joined in holy matrimony, sex will seem natural, effortless, and above all, enjoyable. If you have made the choice to marry her, she obviously must be beautiful in your eyes. Put it this way: would you really need to test-drive a Bentley to decide if you want to own one?

We can all accept that men and women are built differently, both physically and psychologically. These differences, when joined together, can make a beautiful, functional partnership. These differences are to be understood rather than figured out, if that makes any sense. Understand that she may require more from you emotionally than you are used to giving. Understand that your thoughtfulness will impress her more than gift giving. Again, she is not a Rubik's cube to be figured out, she is a human being to be understood. This leads me to the point of what to do during disagreements. They are inevitable, they will happen, and there are ways to deal with them effectively. Most times, an argument will linger days, sometimes weeks between couples, because you have two people attempting to convince each other why they are right and why the other is wrong. In situations like this, sometimes neither person is wrong, it just happens to be all about perspective. For example, if I am standing in Japan, and someone else is standing in America, and the question is asked, "Where is Africa?" My answer would be that Africa is east of me; the other person would answer Africa is to the west. Here you have two different answers; neither is incorrect, but because the position of where we are standing is different, you have an apparent disagreement. Always recognise your perspective when a disagreement arises; this makes it easier to understand the other person's point of view. An argument can be resolved most of the time by two things: a willingness to listen in an attempt to understand rather than to respond, and the laying aside of pride. You may win the fight, and your ego will be boosted, but sometimes it comes at a cost. Value your relationship more than the need to be correct all the time.

Sometimes, she may not want a discussion at all. Sometimes, she may want to vent, be loud, and be upset. It is at this point where she is not looking for you to fix anything. It is in your nature to want to help, but you have to recognise when it is time to offer advice, and when it is time to just listen. She wants to remain true to her feelings, and the worst thing to do is to discredit them.

Most women who have a sense of assurance will not have a problem in letting you play your role. She will recognise the king in you and do what she can to aid and assist you in being the best you possible. Here is a good time to say that she will gladly allow you to be "the man" as long as you demonstrate such qualities. I do not mean you know how to change a flat tyre or replace a blown fuse, but if you understand the importance of her role in your relationship and treat her as your equal, ultimately loving her and making sure she knows it, she will find reciprocating that same energy easy.

If you ever reach the place of realisation during a relationship that things are just not working out, I would strongly advise you to take your time and not make any hasty decisions. A decision that is fuelled with emotion is more often than not the wrong one to make. Everything deserves time and thought. Once you have given your decision all the time it needs, speak to her directly. Be sensitive, and give her clear reasons.

If you find yourself on the receiving end of a break-up, there is no denying it will hurt; trust me, I know. What you must understand about this game called dating is that it is really a process of elimination, leading you to the one you are meant to be with. It will cause you pain for a minute, but never regret or rue a break-up. I am very old school in my methodology when it comes to this subject; if it is meant to be, it will be. As long as both partners put their all into making it work, it will. Having said that, do not let your feelings cloud your judgement. Sometimes, our feelings will have us dive head-first into a situation we know deep down we should not get involved in. Recognise a square peg, round hole situation quickly, and act on it. Delaying this process will only make ripping that band aid off more hurtful.

In choosing a mate, it is important that she is as like-minded as you are. Kings have vision, you want to be able to share that vision with her, and in turn she will be willing to support it. You want to be equally yoked in every area, meaning you want your principles and your values to match with hers. Have more in common than just favourite foods or genre of music. Share a goal and have a plan. All of this takes time, discussion, and clear communication.

She wants to be able to trust you to lead her. She wants to have faith in your ability to make decisions.

What are her ideas about family planning? What does she think about relocating to another country? It is important that you discuss the future together.

One final thing: whatever was the reason you fell in love with her, is going to be the very thing you will rely on to keep the two of you together during difficult times. Do not just seek a woman who ticks all the boxes for you physically. Do not ignore every other quality she has because her lips drip like honey and her hips don't lie. External aesthetic fades; she will not look the same at sixty-five as she did at twenty-five.

Fall in love with the fact she can speak directly to the king in you. Fall in love with the woman who shares your ambition, admires your determination, and wishes the same things for herself. Do not get offended if she challenges you; she just wants the best for you because she knows you are capable. Otherwise, she would not waste her time.

Allow her to be your co-star. You score the goals but let her provide the pass; you score the touchdowns but let her throw the ball to you. She takes a huge sense of satisfaction in playing a part in helping you become great.

She will believe in your vision as long as you will. Coretta Scott King continued the work of her husband, Dr Martin Luther King, long after he died, because she believed in the dream, and she also believed in him.

See yourself as a husband one day. Commitment does not scare kings. Develop the desire to give yourself to one woman; this means you must choose wisely. Be prayerful when decisions need to be made concerning her.

Seek the one who will ultimately trust you, believe in you, sacrifice for you, and above all, love you; it is your duty to do the same for her.

Phase VIII

AM I MY BROTHER'S KEEPER?

"Be slow to fall into friendship; but when thou
art in, continue firm and constant."

Socrates

The two most over-used and misunderstood words in the English language are "love" and "friend."

We throw both these words around like confetti, using them in any context, for any situation, to define any kind of person. They have been exhausted, mistreated, and abused. They have been diluted so much that the real quality of their meaning seems like a foreign concept.

Hip-hop group Whodini released a song entitled *Friends* in the mid-1980s. The opening line is "Friends, how many of us have them?" Good question. A king has advisors, aides, and guards, but what about friends?

Friendship is a bond. A strong one at that. It is the shared mutual affection you have for a person. The formations of friendships are many. A friendship can be birthed in almost any situation or circumstance. There is somewhere in the dynamic of any friendship, something shared, something or someone in common, something they can both undeniably agree on.

The drive to have friends starts from a very early age. Children, once they have learnt how to share, seek other children for the enjoyment of activities. Friendship amongst children is pure and uncomplicated. It is very much "I like Lego, you like Lego, let's be friends." The requirements are simple. Fallouts happen, however, with children. Someone would not let go of the red crayon, tears fall, and children hate each other for a period of four to six minutes before an apology is forced to take place by a parent or guardian. He or she who was aggrieved at not being able to use the red crayon now has it in their possession, and normal friendship is restored. No grudges, no bitterness.

Why, oh why do we have to grow up?

As children get older and enter adolescence, the requirements of friendship become more arduous. Teens now find friendships in shared behaviour just as much as shared interests. I mentioned in an earlier chapter, young people can often have this tendency to conform to a group in an attempt to not be left by themselves, even if this group is to the detriment of their character and their identity. At this stage, the idea of friendship can seem very institutionalised. When it comes to true friendship, a real, authentic bond, it shows neither boundaries nor restraints. True friendship is one of the purest forms of loyalty you can find. It is "no matter what"; it is "under any circumstances." You might have noticed, in modern culture, there is an extreme longing for loyalty from others. This is especially found in young men. There is security, a belonging, a togetherness among both young and older men when together. Men wish to create a bond so tight that they are willing to put this union with other men before everything else. This includes other women, family, and even jobs. While some men do in fact take loyalty and friendship to the extreme, it is important to establish the *right kind of friendship*, with the *right kind of people*, recognising the *right kind of intentions* from others. If you were to honestly assess your circle, in the context of true friendship, you may find that you have very few friends, but countless number of acquaintances. Although it may seem quite depressing to realise, it is absolutely fine, and it is probably where you want to be (I will explain later). There is nothing wrong with having acquaintances. I know you would not refer to someone publicly as such, and it is probably best you don't, but every friendship must start from somewhere. Acquaintances are not people you do not know, they are people you do not know very well on a personal level.

Some people just do not get along. Again, this is a perfectly fine realisation. What you have here is a clash of personalities. If you notice that you have an acquaintance who is making you work a little harder and you are not enjoying their company as much as you thought you would, keep them as an acquaintance, nothing more, and nothing less. What you do not want to do is make an enemy when you know you cannot make a friend. Remember, the goal is to be nice to everyone; if you cannot be nice, be civil, and further still if you cannot be civil, be distant. Say nothing to or about them, and leave it at that.

To class someone as a friend takes more trust than it does time. Just because you may have known someone for years does not qualify them for the title. A friend will always have your best interests at heart. A friend will be truthful in love; they will share your disappointments and celebrate your achievements. A friend will be there when you have fallen and will call time on your period of feeling sorry for yourself. They will gently pull you back when you get too ahead of yourself, but they will allow you to have the limelight without experiencing jealousy.

The right kind of friendship will do so much more for you than just company. Young people feel secure when they have a sense of acceptance. Real friendships bring exactly that: acceptance of you, with all of your faults, failures, and mistakes. Someone who knows your past and does not discredit you for it. An individual who is aware of you at your lowest and still will see enough value in you to want to know you. That is a person worth having around.

The right friendship will help engage you socially. A good friend will help you find other good friends. Some of the greatest friendships often happen by association. This person starts as someone you know because of their relationship with your friend, and over time you begin to see what your friend sees in them and vice versa.

The right kind of friendship will have a positive influence in many areas of your life. Friends often share common interests and goals, and they serve as great motivators. Friendship is more about giving than it is receiving. A friend will sacrifice plenty (within reason) if it means seeing you at a better place than you currently are, without expecting anything in return.

I can understand that at times it can be hard to accept criticism. The difficult part is where the criticism is coming from and what the intentions are. A real friend, however, will never criticise for the sake of it. There may be many in your life who pass judgement and evaluate your every move in an attempt to distract you or unnerve you; some may even do it just to be mean, but someone you share a genuine friendship with will only want to assist you. A friend will challenge you rather than attack you. It is important to know when an enemy is rebuking you and a friend is supporting you, as the two can sometimes sound the very same.

If you class an individual as a friend, then do so with the understanding that a friend should have the capability to defend you at any time. A friend will believe the good in you before they learn of the bad. You will never have to tell a true friend to fight for you, even in your hour of guilt; a friend will do what they can not to leave you exposed to face persecution on your own.

Men love alliances. Men love the idea of being a part of something. Most men will tell you that they take their relationships with their male friends very seriously. You may have heard of a set of rules that male friends must live by: the rule of "brotherly ethics," a "guy code," so to speak. Many of these rules are tongue in cheek, and most go without saying, but they all fall under the umbrella of friendship rule number one: do nothing that will break the trust another has placed in you. It may sound simplistic, but many friendships are strained because the boundaries of the relationship have been challenged. The challenging of such boundaries can be avoided through communication.

A common guy code rule is that friends never date someone another friend has dated before. I can probably say that this is the first unwritten rule many men (and women) abide by. I believe that if you think you are mature enough to date, then you are mature enough to appropriately handle such circumstances. As expressed in a previous chapter, sometimes a relationship does not work out. It is nothing in the long run to get mad or upset about, for it serves as a waste of time and energy fussing over something that cannot be helped. Having said that, a hard part of experiencing a break-up is the thought of that person being happy with someone else; let's be truthful, guys, we hate to admit it, but the image of another succeeding where we failed bugs us.

It is even more painful when you picture that other person being a friend of ours. This scenario is a problem, because from one point of view, it bears no regard for feelings. From the other point of view, there is no longer an attachment, and she is free to date whoever she wants. If we want to talk about conduct between friends, a friend should always bear in mind the emotional attachment that lingers long after a break-up, especially if the relationship was a significant one. A friend should have no problem in communicating their feelings of interest for a person their friend has dated (this I believe is the right thing to do in this instance), and in turn, that friend should be able to effectively and honestly share their opinion. Both friends, however, must take these two points into consideration.

As the one who has experienced the break-up, if you disapprove of your friend dating an ex-partner, you must ask yourself why. The painful truth is just because things did not work out for the two of you, this does not mean it will not for her and someone else, regardless of who that "someone else" is. You cannot void happiness for others while you sit in your own unhappiness. You will probably get all kinds of unpleasant thoughts that will drown your mind about your friend and your ex-partner, especially pre-conceived thoughts about when you were in the relationship. But maturity in this matter will remind you that the feelings you are going through are personal. They are nothing to do with your friend or your ex-partner, and a quick acceptance of the end of the relationship will aid you in moving on. There is no betrayal of trust if your friend came and spoke to you about it; what you may be experiencing is your misery wanting a little company.

If you are the one who has developed feelings for an individual your friend has dated, I cannot stress how important it is to be sensitive to both sets of feelings. You must find the balance of understanding the unhappiness of your friend and seeking happiness of your own. To have a candid conversation with your friend first is the best route to take. Again, be tactful about the words you use and how you use them. It is never a good idea to have these conversations moments after the break-up has occurred. The length of time you should wait is not directly correlated to how long your friend dated, but waiting only a week after they have been dating for years is not using wisdom.

When the time is right, and you can notice a sense of emotional healing in your friend, cautiously approach the subject. Remember, you are not going to ask for his permission. Doing so will leave you with a problem if he turns around and says no. If both of you are honest about how you feel about the situation, there is an amicable resolution to be found that will suit all parties.

I recall a situation between two friends and a pretty, young Portuguese girl back when I was a young teen in school. These two guys were inseparable, the best of friends. Wherever you saw one, you saw the other; as far as a "bro-mance" goes, this was the real thing. One of the guys (let's call him Andrew) developed feelings for this girl who joined the class midway through the year. She had long, curly hair, a huge smile, and an adorable accent. Andrew was smitten; everyone knew how he felt because she was all he could talk about. It didn't take long before Andrew made his move, and just like that, the two were dating. They did everything a young, teenage couple infatuated with each other did; he waited for her after school, they would walk home together, they would send each other text messages all night, they held hands in the playground, she would wear his jacket, and after some time, they became the "it" couple in school. Andrew's friend, however (let's name him Tyrone), was not as happy for his friend as the others were. As a consequence of Andrew's new relationship, his relationship with Tyrone began to suffer. Tyrone became upset with Andrew and accused him of "changing." Andrew accused Tyrone of being jealous, and just like that, a hole appeared at the bottom of their friendship boat. Word began to slowly get out, however, that Tyrone had begun to develop feelings for Andrew's girlfriend. Those rumours were found to be true, as Andrew's girlfriend revealed the text messages she was sent by Tyrone. She was not the innocent party in the middle, as it was also found that she liked Tyrone and was secretly seeing him behind Andrew's back.

One afternoon during the lunch hour, it all took a turn for the worse. Both friends were seen shouting at each other, tensions were high, fists were clenched. They squared up to one another. Tyrone pushed Andrew, and Andrew retaliated and pushed back, and then came the subsequent exchange of swinging fists. Within what seemed like seconds, a crowd formed, and the same look of disbelief was owned by everyone who witnessed the fight. How could two best friends who had known each other for so long come to this? Both young men, filled with anger for each other, allowed pride to take control; for the best part of two years, Andrew and Tyrone did not speak to one another. Andrew's relationship with this young lady ended, and she was even so bold as to date Tyrone for a few months, knowing what had happened between the two former best friends. That relationship did not work out either, and just before the end of our final year at school, she moved back to Portugal. I would love to conclude this story by saying that Andrew and Tyrone put their differences aside and became friends again, but as it sometimes goes, people move on to different things after leaving school, and communication gets lost. Andrew and Tyrone did not keep in contact with each other.

Friendships are great when not met with opposition. But, not for the first time, the opposition between two young men came in the form of a female. I wish I could explain why, but some men (both young and old) lose all sense of time, space, and reality whenever a woman comes into question. Friendships, especially ones that benefit you, are worth holding on to, but sometimes trust is broken, feelings are hurt, and everything you know of each other is tossed directly out of the window, but no relationship is beyond repair. Most apologies are never said because of pride, and forgiveness is never given because of the distress that has been caused. If you are able to put these things aside, and see the friendship as something that can be saved, then save it. Over time you will feel differently about a disagreement, but try not to maintain the same frame of mind you did when you were most emotional. There is so much power in "I'm sorry" and "I forgive you."

Most guy codes are set up to cover a friend's wrong-doings. Men will often set up a scenario of lies that can be verified by their friend. It can even get as deep as a friend making excuses for infidelity. You do not want to build a friendship that is held together by dishonesty. First thing is first. A real friend will never expect you to do anything they know you will be uncomfortable with. I do not buy into the notion of "my mess is your mess." You may feel a sense of obligation to help them in their time of need, and by all means yes, you can help, but you are not helping if you are assisting in fabricating the truth. A rule of friendship, as already discussed, is to always bear in mind the emotional state of your friend. A friend may ask you to do something you are uncomfortable with and, knowing you will be in two minds about it, use your friendship as a bargaining tool. Understand they are not looking out for your emotional state; they are looking out for their own self. It is in a circumstance like this where you must remember who you are.

In every decision you choose to make, do so by checking your integrity. If you believe it could call your integrity into question, throw the red flag and think about it for a second. It does not matter who it is that could be asking you to act dishonestly, but anyone who would willingly jeopardise the royal moral and ethical principles you hold yourself to is someone you do not need to be around. The ultimate decision on any law that needs to be passed in any country belongs to whoever is in charge; whether that is the king, the prime minister, or the president, they have the power to allow something in their kingdom. The same principal belongs to you. Do not become an enabler for dishonesty. A friend may ask something fraudulent of you out of sheer desperation, but you must respond in a way that leaves them still believing they have your support and you still have your integrity.

You have to be as selective in friendship as you are in choosing an outfit for a formal occasion. When we talk about a *real* friend, we are talking about someone who knows and understands you intimately. We are talking about an individual who is freely willing to share himself with you because you both recognise and value of the connection that there is between you. Not everyone deserves to have this description, and not everyone deserves to wear the banner. A friend will prove himself to you time and time again, without any question. Do not feel as though you have to be a friend to everyone. Being a friend to one is work enough; showing care and concern for others is what you want to do, but trying to be a friend to all is unrealistic.

Your circle of friends should above all be trustworthy. It should be water tight, meaning nothing or no one will be able to come between it. Understand that your identity qualifies you to be in the "peculiar" line, and your true friends will stand in line with you. If you want to do better for yourself, it means that your friends at some point will want to do better for themselves also. Your identity attracts; it is a magnet for those who are seeking a sense of self-fulfilment, the same way you are. Knowing you have a dedicated few who are with you for the ride is satisfying; you know they are there because they want to be there. A real friend wants to be a part of your life. They want to share the journey with you and demonstrate to you how much of a friend they can be.

You cannot afford to call everyone "friend," because you cannot afford to take everyone with you. Friendship calls for consistency. And the one thing you want in a friend is solidarity. Anyone who has ever demonstrated changeable, unpredictable, or erratic behaviour towards you is someone you have to think twice about before calling them a true friend. It is hard to place trust in someone who will like you today and be mad at the most frivolous and unimportant thing the next. Life will throw too many arrows at us and bring up our own laundry list of problems without feeling that we are babysitting someone.

Try not to befriend people who always seem to be involved in some kind of drama. There are some people who just seem to attract the wrong kind of attention at all times. Whenever you speak to them, it is one thing after another. They can never seem to find any balance or harmony in their lives. I am not saying to avoid such people, for it is your duty to pray for them and offer any kind of advice should they ask for it, but be discerning about people's intentions. If someone is not bringing anything to the table, you cannot eat with them. Leeches will come in all kinds of innocent and genuine forms, but the reality is there are people who will come into your life to act as a test. Some will come to suck all the energy out of you, some will come to suck all your money from you, some will suck every ounce of patience you have. As long as you remain firm and constant, and remain true to yourself, they will soon exit, as they have nothing else to offer.

At the same time, recognise when someone comes as an addition to your life. As I have pointed out before, friendships are not determined on how long you know a person. Sometimes, on that rare occasion, you meet someone and the two of you get on, as they say, like a house on fire. You connect on a level that only real friends connect on. Again, it is your job to be discerning and wise enough to know who enters your life for a season, and who enters it to stay throughout all seasons. It is okay not to have many friends. One true friend is worth a thousand acquaintances. If you are fortunate to have a true friend in your life, cherish the union you have. Build on it, as it will serve for the foundation of encouragement, comfort, joy, and support should a situation in life happen and you need those things the most. Be your brother's keeper.

You are in each other lives for a special reason. Being equally yoked is not just a term for spouses; it is a term for friends too. To be a king is a lonely position. If you have a friend who understands who you are and will help you achieve all you can be, then that is someone who understands their own royal identity also. Iron sharpens iron. Assist your friends as they assist you. Be there for your friends as they are for you. Love all, and befriend few.

Phase IX

WEARING THE DENTED CROWN

"They can't keep a good man down, always keep a smile when they want me to frown, keep the vibes and I stood my ground, they will never, ever take my crown."

Sizzla Kalonji

Tiger Woods is arguably one of the most successful, decorated, and dominant athletes in the history of professional sports.

Since his arrival into the world of golf at the age of sixteen, Woods has won over a hundred tournaments, held many noteworthy records (including the first golfer in history to hold all four major golf championships at the very same time), and has made over $120 million in prize money from golf alone. Woods has signed endorsement deals with some of the world's biggest brands in the industries of sportswear, cars, luxury watches, and electronics, and he is widely seen as one of the most marketable sportsmen ever.

Woods is also the chair of the Tiger Woods Foundation, a programme that has reached millions of young people all over the world to provide a hands-on, unique learning experience in the areas of mathematics, science, engineering, and sports, to name a few, also creating college and career preparation courses.

Woods is born of an African American father and a Thai mother. His ethnicity has always been made an issue, both on and off the course.

No golfer has been ranked as number one in the world longer than Tiger Woods has, and no golfer has been as consistent as him either.

But for all of his illustrious achievements and accolades, it is regrettable that to many, he will always be known for his extramarital affairs. In 2009, rumours of his infidelity became public; these stories found themselves on the front pages of national newspapers and on the lips of radio and talk show presenters all over the world. Woods released a statement to which he admitted his "transgressions," and this led to more than a dozen women flocking to blogs and TV shows, claiming to have had affairs with him. Woods admitted these allegations and announced that he would be taking an indefinite break from playing golf.

Very quickly after the admission of his misconduct, Woods began to lose his endorsements, and many companies ended the sponsorship deals they had with him. He was dropped from almost every advertising campaign he was involved in and proceeded with a gruelling eight-month divorce case. Woods was even said to be responsible for bringing the game of golf into disrepute. His credibility was in shreds, and a few of his peers in the world of golf began to turn their backs on him. Woods attended a six-week-long therapy programme to help him through his turmoil, before eventually returning to golf in the spring of 2010.

I acknowledge this very intriguing case study, not because of the high profile name, not even because of the apparent scandal of it all, but because it is an astonishing picture of the plight of a man due to bad decisions and poor choices.

As much as some would like to think it does, position does not equate to perfection. Position does, however, attract a higher level of scrutiny.

It is the common quandary of man: the knowledge that perfection is beyond us and our mistakes are forever present. The temptation to move in the dark is a real one, and we sometimes think we will never get caught, not realising that at some point, someone other than ourselves knows where the light switch is. At some point, the dawn comes, and we are left with a case load of evidence against us, with a blinding light shining directly on our shame and embarrassment.

During his statement, Woods revealed that he felt "entitled" to enjoy the temptations that came with his fame. This is an all-too-real statement for most people in prominent positions. A position is dangerous, because it is the perfect cover-up. Who would ever make the man at the top a suspect?

When a situation like this arises, the biggest shock sometimes is not the offence, but it is the offender. Someone who has been trusted with much can in an instant let down so many.

A man is sometimes chosen for a position because he displays the characteristics that will never make him vulnerable to his shortcomings. Many see his reliance, monitor his dependence, and watch him build up his credit of integrity. Power gives you exactly that: power. Authority can cloud judgement, and integrity takes the back seat behind supremacy. When people learn that a man is not who his position suggests him to be, the repercussions are dire. Power is when your direct decisions no longer have an impact on just you and your livelihood; everyone who is connected and affiliated with you suffers to a degree from your decisions. Should there really be a distinction between the transgressions made by someone in Woods' position and those made by the man whose name you do not know who hands out free newspapers at the train station? In an ideal world, there should not be, as at the end of the day, when the smoke has cleared and the dust has settled, we will all have to give an account for the life we have lived, and we will all be judged on one level playing field. But as of right now, this is the problem of the platform.

Perfection is absolute. It is spotless, stainless, unblemished, and untarnished. It is everything we are not. As flawed as we are, there is this need to appear blameless before everyone else. We do not want anyone to lay witness to our weaknesses and failures. The strain of keeping up this kind of appearance will only continue to remind us of how sketchy we really are, thus leaving us open to making bad decisions and poor choices. As long as we have the capabilities to say and do the wrong thing, given the right circumstance, there will always be a tendency to do exactly that.

There is also the flip side to this unclean coin. Some may realise that we are so imperfect that any kind of attempt to make any improvement in our behaviour is pointless, so we will knowingly do what we see to be the wrong thing without any fear of accountability. Either way, it is a mentality we must rid ourselves from.

A king in charge of a country can never make a decision that will not benefit the people he oversees first. When we think of his role, he must remain in a state of readiness to serve the people. If only we maintained this line of thought when we make the decisions that we do. Why is it that our capabilities to fail and do wrong can overwhelm our capabilities to succeed and do well?

We can easily lose sight of how much what we do affects those around us. Our mind suggests that when there is no one around, there is no need to perform. Knowing we have the ability to do wrong, we will willingly do it (and sometimes without guilt). This is mainly because, number one, it is in us to do it, and number two, there is no one around to pass judgement. It is the easiest thing in the world to do right when everyone is looking, but how do you pass up the temptation of getting what you want, knowing you can, when the process of getting it is dishonest?

You will always hear people say that you should not care what people think about you, and that is true. I have said exactly this in a previous chapter; what this refers to is an opinion that has been manufactured, one that has been created falsely to cause harm to you. *That* opinion you should take no notice of. But what about an opinion of you that is justified? The opinion made of you when all the evidence is against you and has found you to be guilty? I would say it is this opinion you ought to care about. You ought to care about the presumption of a loved one when you have been found to be deceiving. You ought to take to heart the feelings of someone close to you when you have behaved in an unscrupulous manner. The reason I say this is the fact that your actions form assessments. You cannot get mad at someone who thinks a certain way about you due to the behaviour that *you* have displayed. It is up to you how you want to be viewed; it is not in your best interests to appear lackadaisical about the thoughts towards you from others. To throw your hands in the air and show no regard to how you are thought of because of your actions speaks of a person with questionable character. I am not saying that you should do good just so people will think you are, but think about how you conduct *yourself* in a world where under-the-table tactics and behind-the-back business is performed; you will find favour when others can see you have decided to be forthright for yourself when you are in a position when the easy way out is to do the wrong thing.

The negative thoughts and opinions of others towards you can make you do one of two things: it can leave you in a quagmire of your own flaws, or it can be the step ladder you need to make better decisions. There is a tendency to do bad because "they already think I am bad, so one more bad choice will not make them think any less of me."

This is a lie. You can use this as a way to prove not just to others, but to yourself, that you are capable of doing well and you are capable of righting your wrongs. Everyone is apt to slip up, but so many stay on the ground and give others no choice but to think that is where they belong. It is on you to recognise your slip and learn from it, meaning see how you slipped, why you slipped, and what you can do to make sure you do not slip again.

My favourite jazz artist of all time, Miles Davis, once said, "When you hit a wrong note, it is the next note you hit that counts." How powerful and appropriate this statement is. In musical terms, a succession of incorrect notes will leave the listener believing the artist is ill-prepared, ill-disciplined, and not very good at their craft. He or she may never get another opportunity to play in front of a crowd again and sabotage their chances of ever selling records. But if the next note they play, and the notes thereafter, are the right ones after the incorrect one, it will be clear to every listener that it was a simple mistake, one that is easily made, and one that will be forgotten because the subsequent notes are played perfectly.

It is your choice as to how you play out the next scenario in your life after a mistake. Making mistakes, big or small, can cause you to lose focus. It can cause you to take your eyes off the bigger picture and have you stuck in the moment of error. But do you keep playing? Do you acknowledge that error as a "whoops" moment and continue as you know how, or do you fill your mind with guilt and concern, wondering if anyone heard that bum note, wondering if they will see you as an amateur, wondering if anyone will come out to see you play again. They say that perception is reality, and it is easy to see yourself as your mistake. But as mentioned in a previous chapter, your behaviour is activity, and activity is not identity. Your mistake is what you have done, it is not who you are. After you hit the wrong note, does that mean you are no longer an artist? Does it mean you no longer know how to play? Do you want to be defined as your wrong note, or are you an artist who, like every artist before and after you, hit a bad note, but kept on playing?

Long after others may have forgiven us of our mistakes, we can still be in the place of useless thought because we have not forgiven ourselves. Our mistakes can cause us so much shame and embarrassment; we often stay in this frame of mind as a method to punish ourselves. Self-condemnation can have a devastating effect on what we see when we look in the mirror. When we pass sentence on ourselves in such an extreme way, we become like the prisoner sitting in the cell when the door is wide open and we have been given clearance to leave. What we must do in a situation like this, is put everything into perspective and see it for what it exactly is. We are never above a mistake in life, regardless of its severity, and at the same time, redemption is always within our reach, even if we think we have sunken to the very bed of the ocean floor.

We lose in life when we do not learn. An apparent loss is simply a moment of education. That education is more often than not receiving punishment for our wrongs. Punishment is not negative if you look at it from a different lens. It is correction; it reminds you that you had no business turning left when you were instructed to stay on the straight road. If you use your mistakes to your advantage, you can actually arrive at the place of understanding a lot faster had you not have gone through the experience of making a mistake.

A mistake does not mean expiration, and failure is not final. They serve as a part of a chapter in the book of your life.

As a football fan, I have always known Manchester United to be the dominant force in English football. In my generation, they have been the standout team that has won numerous trophies, both domestically and in Europe. They were the team that everyone feared, the team no other team liked to play. It was always a surprise when they lost a game, but it was the biggest bombshell when they were beaten badly. I recall an interview with Alex Ferguson, the head coach of the team at the time, after one of their worst losses in recent memory. United, champions at the time, travelled to play Southampton, a team who were struggling to score goals let alone win a game. United lost to them, however, which was a surprise to everyone. Ferguson said after the game, "The true test of a champion is not what you do when you are winning, but it is how you react after a defeat."

I found out that four of Manchester United's heaviest defeats in the Premier League all came in seasons where they ended up being crowned champions.

We all fall short of our own expectations and make decisions outside of our character; this time calls for us to be level headed. It may feel like it at the time, but our mistakes do not mean the world stops revolving and the stars come crashing down. This time calls for us to see our shortcomings without defending them. We may have to endure a season of ridicule, disappointment, and isolation, and as strange as it sounds, we will look back on that moment with a sense of gratitude when we see where we are if we have used the experience to our advantage. It probably took Manchester United an embarrassing defeat to realise they are not immortal, and they used the negative of that situation to correct whatever lapse in concentration they may have had. The same must be applied to us. Our mistakes serve as reminders for us, to say that we are not above the law, we are flawed, but the bigger picture remains in spite of our imperfection.

As a teenager, I played on a football team that was on a horrible losing streak. It seemed as if every week, regardless of the opponent, we just had a feeling we would lose. We made all the excuses under the sun for our failures; if we conceded first, we would drop our heads, point fingers at each other, and accept we were the worst team in the entire league. Early one windy Sunday morning, we travelled to play one of the best teams in the city. In those days, both teams had to share a dressing room, and the trash talk from the other team began the moment we walked in. Needless to say, we had nothing in terms of retaliation. Once the game kicked off, however, it was a different story. We matched them stride for stride until we took the lead just before halftime. They did everything to get back into the game, but to no avail. We won the game by a single goal. We could not enjoy the victory until long after the final whistle, because we were too exhausted to celebrate. We gave everything we had. We ran, ran, and then ran some more. That game sparked a winning streak that lasted almost an entire season.

I tell that story all the time as a point that it seemed easier to maintain a winning streak than it was to snap a losing one. It was all in our mindset and attitude. We could not see past our loss, we embodied it in our identity, and as a consequence we played like losers. It took a monumental effort to buck the trend, but once we did, we found winning natural.

We all make mistakes, but it is important to not develop a mentality of wrongdoing, where our first thought is always to do what we see as the wrong thing. If we do make a misjudgement, it is vital we recover quickly, shake off any guilt, and dust off any dirt that resembles self-condemnation.

We must learn to set ourselves in a state of correction whenever we make bad decisions and poor choices. There are only so many times you can trip over your own untied shoelaces before you actually fall and seriously hurt yourself. Kings have been dethroned, rulers have lost their heads, and prime ministers have been expelled from their positions because of dishonesty. Using these examples as an extreme case, we have been given a chance to redeem ourselves from our mishaps.

It is the mentality of so many to overlook the hundreds of things you did right for the one thing you did wrong. What is important is that you do not lose sight of who you really are when others wish to make it as clear as day that you are not who your position suggests you are.

Mistakes can be common to the one who knows he is flawed, but respect is due to the one who desires to make his second chance count. All of us have been given this opportunity to live honestly, and while some people may point to the fact that you have fallen once before, let the next move you make be a reminder that your determination to be better than the person you were yesterday counts for more than your shortcomings.

I know what it feels like to have dropped your crown. I know what it is like to have people see you drop it and kick it as you attempt to pick it up. When you do eventually pick up your crown, you will notice all the damage that has been done to it. You cannot hide the dents, you cannot buff out the scratches, all you can do is wipe it down and put it back on your head. To be given a new one is not an option. We have to live with the one that was dropped. People will point fingers and laugh amongst themselves at the condition of your crown, but do not lose sight in the fact you still have one. A dented crown is like having battle scars; it says to the viewer that you have been in a fight; you may have taken a few losses and come out worse for wear, but they forget that you have come out alive. They forget that they cannot take your crown from you; this is why you are constantly reminded of how many dents yours has.

Yes, you are imperfect, but you are still a king. Use every opportunity you get to improve, not for anyone else's benefit, but simply for your own. Tiger Woods found himself in the deepest of valleys. He could blame no one but himself for it too. While many did their best to keep him there, he recognised his inadequacy and took steps to be a better man. When Woods returned to golf, it did not take him long to get back to the ranking of the number one golfer in the world.

Pick your crown up and wear it. Use your mistakes as a testimony to others that even when you have fallen, it is never too late to pick yourself up. Keep going. This time, move with more care and caution. King Solomon once said a just man falls seven times and gets back up again. You are not perfect, but God is, and it is He who gave you your crown. Not the man who highlights your faults, but the God who looks beyond them.

Phase X

THE PRAYER

"Men always ought to pray, and not lose heart."

Luke 18. 1

*H*eavenly Father,

    You made us male, you ordained us kings. As we look in the mirror, we see man before us. Flesh, bone, and skin. Strong but flawed. Called, but unwilling. When you look at us, through and beyond what we can see, you see the truth. We are, because of you. You called us your finest. The creation you formed with your very hands. The dust of the ground was your only resource. Your breath was enough to give us life. Your plan for us was written before time can be fathomed. We are not close to being deserving of you, we are the worst candidates, but you saw enough in us for a purpose only you can sew together.

For some reason, you are mindful of us. For some reason, you care. For some reason, you love. You created a throne for us before we were a thought and gently placed us on its plush, heavenly cushioning before we could form sentences. As you watched us grow older, you shook your head at our disobedience and frowned at our unreasoning, but you left us on our throne. You hated our sinfulness, and our behaviour was indignant towards you, but you left us on our throne. You believed us even when we told no truths and defended us when we were guilty.

And yet, you still saw us fit for the job and continued to call us by what you saw: chosen; royal; holy; different. If only we can see through your eyes for just a mere moment, even for a glimpse, a peek is all I ask, for your ways are beyond me. Who I see before me is not suited for the position. My environment says otherwise, my family says otherwise, my transgressions say otherwise. All I can do is take a deep breath, close my eyes, and trust that when I jump, you will catch me.

This purple robe you have given me fits me perfectly, but it looks better on someone else. This throne you have given me is comfortable, but I feel too exposed. I cannot understand a place so honourable for a person so undeserving. My trials are what you want me to go through. My pain is who you would have to keep me humble. My experiences are who you have selected to teach me. My identity is who you have made me to be. So who am I? I'm whatever you say I am. Made in the image of you, in the image of the King. So I stand with the countless number of kings around the world, in agreement with the plan and the purpose you have set for our lives. We have been called to live in the understanding of who we are. Forgive those who thought we are emotionless, weak characters. Pardon the few who assumed we are our clothes, our culture, and our past. Have mercy on those who wished we would be quiet and sit in the corner like good little boys and wait for our turn to speak. Excuse the individuals who dismissed our dreams and highlighted our fears. Overlook the ones who caused us physical pain. Exempt those who scarred our emotions, and bear no malice on the people who swore against our destiny. We want to overcome obstacles and build houses with the bricks the enemy has thrown at us. We want to demonstrate strength in our very being. We want to carry confidence and faith in each arm while stepping on scorpions and snakes while goodness and mercy follows us. As long as we are here, we want our sisters to fear not. We desire our queens to have assurance in us. As long as we are here, we want them to be covered. We wish to be the foundations our children stand on. We want to be such an example that they do better and go further than we could ever go. Let us be so focused on the task you have set before us that we have no time to address those who speak ill. Camouflage our hearts, harbour our minds, conceal our thoughts, and let our soul find a sanctuary in you so that we do not become distracted and fall off course. Let us not develop a lust for the things of this world. Help us to not let the minor become major, and the major become minor. Help us to easily recognise what is important, simplify the task at hand, and grant us clarity of judgement. Never let us feel the need to impress, keep us from wanting to show off, and hold us back from making a spectacle of ourselves.

Help us to be grateful for the past, thankful for the present, and excited about the future. In every moment of pain, confusion, disappointment, hurt, and anguish, remind us of the bigger picture. Give us a good word for someone in their time of need, and help us to be a blessing to strangers. Remind us always that prayer accompanies us in the process, humility stands as a priority, worship is involved in the purpose, and integrity is a part of the staple. Having done all to stand, we will keep standing. We will tear up the paper given to us by society that has been rubber stamped with the word "stereotype" and toss it in the air like confetti to celebrate these kings.

We will put you first, we will live and not die, we will succeed even when we have tasted failure, and we will trust you to attend to our business as we attend to yours. We shall overcome, we will make it, and we will give you the glory. Let us see our identity for our own sake. Thank you for the chance to live as you intended us to: chosen, royal, holy, different. You made us male; you ordained us kings.

Thank you. In Jesus' name.

Amen.

Finale

YOU ARE IMPORTANT

There is currently a war being raised against our young men.

From the days of Moses, where Pharaoh ordered the murder of every male child, to our current situation of relentless violence and purposeless lives, this sustained attack on our youth cannot be purely a coincidence.

"Regicide" is the term for the deliberate execution of a king. Monarchs have been killed in the past as an attempt to overthrow power. The perpetrator understands that if you remove the king, you remove order, authority, and influence.

Call me super spiritual, but we have an enemy who is very aware that if these young men were to ever understand who they are, if they were to ever realise their true identities, the world would be transformed for the better. They say the only way to be sure that something is truly dead is to cut off the head, and this is what is happening. Our societies are dying because our boys are being cut off; our future leaders are being dispossessed of their purpose. The graves and the prisons are full, but the thrones are empty.

This is the picture of importance that our young brothers possess. You are important. So important that the devil would like nothing more than to see you fail and become nothing; this would mean one less soul finding his identity, and one less soul coming into relationship with the One who gave it to him.

I don't care how you feel about yourself, I don't care about the mistakes you may have made, I don't even care if you still don't believe you are a king, but you have to believe you are significant. You have to believe you are important.

They say that each of the four kings in a deck of playing cards represents a specific historical figure. The king of spades is said to be King David. The same David who was the least of his brothers. The same David who wasn't much of a thought in the eyes of his own father. The same David who cleaned up after animals. The same David who wasn't "important." This David was handpicked, chosen, and selected. His anointment came before his appointment. He was guided in his gifting before he performed from his position. He didn't know it, and his family didn't think of it, but all this time, there was a king on the inside of the kid.

David didn't always make the wisest decisions, but he accomplished some of the most amazing things any human being has done in their time on this earth. David trusted God in the bad times, and in the bad times God reminded David of his identity. He found the strength to encourage himself when life didn't look favourable and kept on with the pursuit of his purpose when situations told him not to.

David was dealt a hand, and he played it. You, too, are dealt a hand, and it's up to you to play yours.

If David were alive today, he probably wouldn't look much different than a lot of us. He would have probably struggled with the same issues and insecurities that we do. But I'm glad he went before us, because he is an example that we indeed can be who God has called us to be.

Maybe it's merely a coincidence, maybe it's intentional, but the spade, out of all four suits in a deck of cards, is said to be most powerful and dominant.

You would have never guessed the way his life began as a child that "powerful" and "dominant" would be words synonymous with David, but the least and the weak are always used to confront the strong and the mighty.

Have you ever had feelings of being insignificant? Have you ever felt like you just didn't matter? I know I have, but the one thing I have realised is that the more you begin to invest in yourself (meaning seeing yourself as someone of importance, treating yourself as someone with value and purpose), the more you will begin to understand that what is on the inside of you is worth more than what's on the outside.

Our insignificance will always compare us to others. We will never think we are good enough, because there is always someone better than us. But don't let this be an excuse; sometimes you have to keep playing, even if you're the only one who thinks you're good enough. If no one ever pats you on the back, if no one ever congratulates you or applauds you, never forget to celebrate yourself.

Everyone expects the king to remain strong. They expect the king to be fearless. I want to remind you that in the moments of weakness and doubt, seek God for strength, wisdom, and direction, then go back outside and face the world with confidence, believing that you indeed are "the man."

I want to encourage you to seek to be a real man, not what you see on TV; society tells us that being a man is connected to what is in your bank account, what kind of car you drive, the fact you can lift seventy kilograms at a time, and you never shedding a tear.

Being a man is embracing what God has put on the inside of you.

My brother, there is so much more for you. Your life matters. You are not just a man. You are not just your skin colour. You are important. You are special. You are loved. You are needed. You are different. You are unique. You are noble. You are significant. You are powerful. You are strong. You are brave. You are smart. You are anointed. You are king.

The time is now. Put on your crown, adjust your robe, and possess your throne. If you play your cards right, there is no telling what life has in store for you. I love you. I'm proud of you.

Breathe in. Breathe out. Ready? Let's go and be great.

#King

Igitur Perfecti!

About the Author

Julien Mitchell is a licensed minister of the Calvary Church of God in Christ, UK. Born and raised in East London, he was inspired and motivated by his own upbringing to write a book addressing the matter of self-identity among young men.

He works locally and nationally with the church and is active in the areas of youth development and Sunday school. He is a coveted conference speaker and teacher, which has seen him travel nationally as well as internationally. He currently holds three degrees in the fields of journalism, semiotics, and creative writing.